How to Become a
Professional
Travel Writer

Advice from 50 years of
international assignments

Mark Eveleigh & Narina Exelby

For Lucia,
who has been our favourite travelling companion
(and tireless researcher) since the tender age
of eight.

ABOUT THE AUTHORS

Mark Eveleigh and Narina Exelby have racked up a combined total of almost 50 years in what they still consider to be the world's most exciting business.

Their paths merged from very different backgrounds... After completing a Bachelor of Arts degree and a Post Graduate Diploma in Journalism, Narina worked full-time on some of the most well-known travel and lifestyle magazines in the UK and South Africa. Mark dropped out of formal education and, although he didn't realise it at the time, the following decade as a backpacker and 'explorer' (leading expeditions in various parts of Asia, Africa and Latin America) was a sort of apprenticeship during which he travelled extensively, researched and read voraciously, and studied three languages.

Narina and Mark met briefly for a cappuccino in London in 2001 when she was a travel editor and he a freelance writer, but it wasn't until 11 years later that they became a unit. They spent the next three years travelling permanently from assignment to assignment, living out of their kitbags in various parts of Europe and

Asia, and often out of an expedition-prepared Land Rover in Africa.

In a normal year Narina and Mark tend to spend around six months on the road. Freelance travel writing provides the perfect lifestyle for incurable nomads and until the Covid-19 lockdown 'trapped' them in Indonesia it had been eight years since the couple had spent three weeks in one place. These days they base themselves in Narina's hometown in South Africa and at the two beach houses they built in West Bali, where Narina writes and practises yoga and Mark's writing bouts are dictated by high-tide surf-sessions.

Between them, Mark and Narina have written travel features for more than 150 publications, including *National Geographic, BBC Wildlife, BBC Travel, CNN Travel, The Telegraph, The Independent, The Guardian, Esquire, Sports Illustrated, Conde Nast Traveller, Africa Geographic, Getaway, Sunday Times Travel Magazine, CNN Traveller, The Boston Globe, Lonely Planet, Women's Health, Atlanta Journal-Constitution, Wanderlust, South China Morning Post, National Geographic Traveller and National Geographic Adventure.* They have also contributed to the inflight magazines of British Airways, KLM, Emirates, Qatar, Qantas, Kenyan Airways, Korean Airlines, Garuda, Singapore Airlines, Gulf Air, Uganda Airways, Malaysian Airlines and Philippine Airlines.

Having published well over 1,200 full-length travel features between them, Mark and Narina are considered to be among the most widely published freelance travel journalists in the industry.

CONTENTS

FOREWORD

'If we cover all expenses, fly you business-class from London and guarantee to buy three features, how soon could you head off to Tasmania for us?'

The voice at the other end of the line came from the offices of England's best-selling travel magazine and the only reason I delayed my response was because my cell-phone signal suddenly disintegrated into a blast of static caused by the sandstorm that raged outside my tent in Oman's Empty Quarter.

Many writers (and countless bloggers and influencers) have paid homage to the idea of 'travelling for free'. But the dream is usually a fleeting one and, in most cases, it ends with a rude wake-up call when the savings run out and the dreamers are forced to wake up to a 'proper job'.

I know how that feels.

I dropped out of formal education with no ambition beyond a vague wish to 'see the world'. To finance that ambition I spent around six months of each year driving lorries, brewery trucks and courier vans, or working as a farmhand, doing house removals, driving dumpsters or laying concrete on airport construction jobs. I also did door-to-door sales (flogging oil paintings and perfume), fitted water-meters and worked night shifts as a forklift driver in a gigantic freezer, where the temperature fluctuated around -40°C and snowflakes drifted from the lofty ceiling. It was possibly this latter experience that provoked an enduring fondness for the tropics. To this day I rarely take assignments in places where I might require a coat.

After several years I got into the habit of searching out casual work as a security guard, because it allowed ample time to research and read. I was far from a dedicated security guard, invariably clocking on for duty with a copy of *In Patagonia* or *The Great Railway Bazaar* tucked into my bag and a folded sheet of Indonesian, Spanish or French vocabulary in my back pocket (to be memorised in preparation for whatever trip was on the horizon).

An obsessive bibliophile for as long as I can remember, I read everything relating to travel, from Joseph Conrad and W. Somerset Maugham to Redmond O'Hanlon and Paul Theroux. Eric Newby and William Dalrymple would have me dreaming of distant lands when I was supposed to be concentrating on CCTV screens. But Hemingway and Laurie Lee were my literary heroes and, when 84-hour working weeks threatened my sanity, they frequently conspired to lure me onto mid-summer hitchhiking trips to the Spanish Sierras.

Even in my earliest travels it had seemed natural to hunt out remote corners that didn't merit coverage in the guidebooks. In Guatemala I rented a hut and a horse and rode through the northern jungles, far beyond Tikal Ruins, looking for jaguars. In Morocco I hitch-hiked to a desert enclave to spend Christmas (mine was almost certainly the only 'Christmas' in town) surrounded on three sides by

Algerian machine-gun nests. In Venezuela I almost died in a cable-car accident (two other people did) while on a mission to travel through the high Andes with a mule.

It was back in 1995 that my first travel feature was published and I stumbled my way into freelance travel writing as a career. I'd like to say that it had always been my dream job, but the reality is that I'd never imagined that such a job even existed. I consider myself incredibly lucky to have been living that dream now for over a quarter of a century.

This book won't teach you how to be a travel writer; it will teach you how to become a professional travel writer. And that is an entirely different bag of tricks.

There are many different paths that could lead to success as a travel writer and we can only explain the ones that we've taken – the roads less travelled, perhaps. For this reason, it is necessary at times to outline our own specific experiences. Through these sections (described as 'been there…' sections in the text) we hope that the reader will have a chance to benefit as much from the frequent stumbling blocks in our careers as from decisions that have led to successful and lucrative assignments.

The tips outlined in this book – the fruits of half a century of assignments – will help you to get your first work published. This book will explain how to entice the clients whose paycheques will continue to fund a whole string of once-in-a-lifetime trips. It will also clue you in on the potential pitfalls in establishing ongoing working relationships with the PR companies, tour operators or hotel owners who can get you on location and into a position to research your articles.

If travel writing is your dream job this book could turn

you into a fulltime pro. If, on the other hand, freelance writing merely strikes you as a wonderful way to supplement your income it will teach you skills that could benefit you throughout life, no matter what other career choices you make.

Travel journalism is one of the world's most competitive businesses, and this book doesn't set out to sugar-coat what can, for the faint-hearted, become a bitter pill. There can be few other careers where thousands of people would happily queue for an opportunity to work for free… or for 'exposure' as it's known in the publishing world. Even after having almost 1,000 full-length features published, I'm constantly haunted by the masses who would do my job gratis – for the inestimable pleasure of a free trip to their dream destination… or even just for the thrill of seeing their names in print.

In an average year I publish around 40 or 50 full-length travel features and with every confirmed commission that lands in my inbox (with a serious, professional payrate attached) my faith is renewed in the fact that editors will always need professional writers.

There is magic in writing. This book will show you how to harness that magic and, having done so, it will guide you along a no-nonsense path to getting your work published and consolidating your position in one of the world's most exciting careers.

Mark Eveleigh
KwaZulu-Natal, South Africa
July 2021

1

WHAT IT TAKES TO BE A PROFESSIONAL TRAVEL WRITER

by Narina Exelby

*Talent is cheaper than table salt.
What separates the talented
individual from the successful one is
a lot of hard work.*

— Stephen King —

There's a lot more to being a professional travel writer than swanning around the world at someone else's expense. More often than not, it's initially at your own expense – and there's a lot of behind-the-scenes work that goes into making each trip profitable. A typical freelance travel writer spends less time on actually writing than on chasing and securing commissions, setting up trips, liaising with editors, researching, editing (and captioning) photographs, working as their own IT guru, accountant or PA... In other words, there's a lot more to being a travel writer than simply travelling and writing.

If you want to know exactly how the timeframe of a commissioned assignment tends to come together then skip to chapter 4 – but there's a lot to understand before you reach the point where you're ready to start filling that first blank page with words. This chapter will equip you with the tools you need to find your own style, rhythm and ways of working.

THE QUALITIES OF A PROFESSIONAL TRAVEL WRITER

Everyone's going to bring their own skills and quirks to the job but there are a few traits that make some people more suited than others to thriving on the life of a pro freelance travel writer.

BE OKAY WITH UNCERTAINTY

Life as a travel writer is often unpredictable. If you're prepared for this and know from the very start that it's always going to be a rollercoaster, you'll learn to thrive on the ride.

Some months will be quiet in terms of workflow, while others will be absolutely manic. Your monthly income might vary wildly (see chapter 9 for information on how the finances work). Some months will be jam-packed with travel, while others might be more sedentary but crammed with 14-hour working days. There will be months where you need to beat tight deadlines while simultaneously focusing on the planning of new assignments. That's just the way it is – be okay with it or burn out fast.

BE TENACIOUS

There will be weeks – many weeks, sometimes – when you are close to panic because editors seem to have forgotten that you exist and you don't even get a reply to your pitches. Your bank balance is running low, you just can't get that story to come together and you seem to be running into roadblocks every step of your way. When those times arrive – and they will – remind yourself why you wanted to become a travel writer in the first place… and soldier on with the assurance that better times are on the horizon.

BE FLEXIBLE

This is a big one. Plans can change – often at very short notice – so you need to be open to making a last-minute trip, or to rescheduling your social or family life in order to meet a tight deadline. If you prefer to work regular hours and keep weekends and holidays free, then you're likely to find that opportunities for work can be quite limited. The easier you can make life for editors, the more likely you are to become their go-to contributor.

Having the flexibility to change your plans will make life easier for you too – because being a freelance travel writer is as much a lifestyle as it is a career choice. Shifting plans and logistics at short notice can be stressful but having the freedom to say 'yes' – to trips, assignments, adventures – is arguably one of the biggest perks of being a freelance travel writer.

Been there, says Mark...

As I started to outline the chapters in this book, I was on assignment on a private nature reserve in South Africa when Mother Nature threw a curve ball.

I'd been commissioned to write a cover feature for a major UK newspaper, and the day before I was due to drive into Kruger National Park to begin a week-long camping trip, a tropical cyclone began to wreak havoc across the region. Rivers broke their banks, bridges washed away, camp sites were closed and people were fleeing the very parts of the park I was due to visit.

I had two options: throw in the towel and head home (not feasible, as I'd then have to cancel a lucrative commission and disappoint a valued client); or sit the storm out and postpone the safari for at least a week. The lodge owners on the private reserve generously offered me a bed while I waited for the weather to clear, and I gratefully accepted the chance to stay dry and make use of the good Wi-Fi connection. You see, it wasn't as simple as shifting dates out by a week because after the camping trip I was booked into three other lodges, so I had to take their availability into account when I changed plans.

Suddenly a trip that had taken a month to organise had to be rearranged in three days amid frantic juggling of logistics as I liaised with three lodges, four PR agencies, one AirBnb host, one 4x4 vehicle-hire company, and changed bookings at five camp sites. It was a crazy domino-game of plans and bookings that eventually fell into place and, thanks to a wonderfully responsive PR contact, I was able to build in an unexpected stay at a brand-new lodge – and that lead to two additional features being commissioned.

Flexibility helps, big time.

BE INSATIABLY CURIOUS

The more you read and research and dig and explore, and the more people you meet and questions you ask, the more you're going to uncover on your travels. This not only leads to a wider variety of angles for features, but it will also deepen your understanding of a place – and that's crucial when it comes to travel writing. Reading, researching, digging, exploring, tasting, engaging, listening – these add so many potential layers to your stories. And balance that tenacity with open-mindedness because the most obvious story is rarely the most interesting one.

BE A GOOD LISTENER

Having the ability to keep quiet and keep someone else talking is frequently the best way to tease out a story.

Occasionally someone will come up with a quotable statement or anecdote that is such a gem, you realize that this particular story is almost going to write itself.

Gently listening to what people have to say – their opinions, observations and beliefs – will often encourage them to open up to you. Develop a sense of trust and they might give you insight into what could be an even more powerful background story.

You owe it to the people who take the time to share their thoughts and experiences to listen carefully and report accurately and with sensitivity. Treat their personal stories with humility because without their input you would have no story to tell. French philosopher Michel de Montaigne summed it up beautifully (way back in 1595): 'I have gathered a posy of other men's flowers and nothing but the thread that binds them is mine own.'

It is easy to dig for second-hand research on the Internet, but the original thoughts you harvest first-hand from experts or people who've lived in an area for decades will be what makes your work original in comparison to your lazy cut-and-paste competitors.

HAVE AN OPEN MIND

There's no shortage of inspirational quotes about how travel opens the mind. As a travel writer, however, you need to begin your journey with a mind that is *already* open.

Of course, you'll have ideas about the angles you're wanting to chase for a feature, but going into it with rigid, preconceived ideas is very limiting and can often mean that you'll overlook what could be the most interesting aspects of your story. The travel industry is rife with clichéd generalizations: Venice of the East; Manhattan of Latin America; Paris of the Orient. Try not to fall into these traps (either in your writing or in your thinking) because these clichés do no real justice to truly unique destinations that have a peculiar fascination all their own… and might frequently be far more appealing even than Venice, Manhattan or Paris.

It's a natural reaction upon arrival in a new place for us to try to categorize it and fit it into pigeonholes, but these sentiments are like blinkers that stop you from looking beyond shallow first impressions to a wider reality. Block any thoughts that go along the lines of 'oh, this reminds me of the Masai Mara / Venezuela / Ulaanbaatar…' since they stop you from accepting a place for what it is. Every new destination will have its own unique magic, if you look hard enough and keep an open mind.

Been there, says Mark…

I was once sent to Vasco da Gama in Goa to do a city report on what the editor warned me was a 'grungy, dirty, uninteresting urban mess'… but I stayed there so long that I fell in love with the city and had to write a completely different story.

'Vasco da Gama had caught my attention from the moment I first saw it on the map,' I wrote in a story that ran under the title Good Times in Vasco da Gama. *'During the*

long journey south from Kashmir to Delhi, onwards through Rajasthan and past Mumbai, the city seduced me with its mystery. It intrigued me all the more since, despite being Goa's largest city, it did not warrant even a mention in my guidebooks.'

§

2

WHAT TO EXPECT FROM A CAREER ON THE ROAD

by Mark Eveleigh

My writing is a combination of three elements. The first is travel: not as a tourist but travel as exploration. The second is reading literature on the subject. The third is reflection.

– Ryszard Kapuściński –

When I started freelancing in the mid-1990s my articles were written double-spaced on a typewriter and then snail-mailed to editors along with a package of captioned and labelled slides. Even in later years, when email came into use, there were years of complicated assignments where deadlines had to be adjusted to allow for the time needed to get slides duplicated, packaged and dispatched. I still recall anxious hours spent in backpacker hostels in San Jose, Harare and Delhi waiting for couriers to collect my precious packages of images.

Despite these complications, we travel writers considered ourselves fortunate to be able to work remotely. The Internet had given us access to the greatest information resource the world had ever known (with caveats, see chapter 8) and we were able to file the text for our stories without delay.

Earlier travel writers and foreign correspondents needed either dedicated agents or reserves of private funds to be able to work from the road. (As Hemingway well knew, a series of wealthy wives was also useful.) A few relatively impoverished writers stand out from the crowd, like the unsung hero Ryszard Kapuściński, who emerged from a Polish ghetto to start a career as one of the world's greatest international reporters. Arriving in Africa from Warsaw in the 1950s, Kapuściński had felt immediately at home because 'food was scarce there too and everyone was also barefoot'.

Times have certainly changed (these days even fewer newspapers have budgets to maintain foreign correspondents on location) and technology has made it easier than ever to work from anywhere, even in the world's most undeveloped areas.

It was not until 2004 that I finally became convinced that digital cameras had advanced to the point where most editors would take them seriously. Suddenly there was an opportunity to work much more effectively from anywhere in the world. The ability to be able to communicate across the planet almost instantly was a benefit that the pioneers of travel writing could never have imagined. Communications progressed rapidly and by 2009 I was able to spend an entire month working out of a Land Rover in the Ugandan bush, charging my equipment with a plug-in inverter, and filing articles and photos via a satellite phone.

TRAIN YOURSELF TO
WORK FROM ANYWHERE

We live in an era when large numbers of people have been forced to come to terms with working from home. Many have found it a harrowing experience, but many more have embraced the sense of freedom that comes from working remotely. There's something to be said for substituting a strap-hanging commuter trip to the office for a sedate barefoot shuffle to the kitchen table.

Some people have found it challenging to remain motivated day after day when their time is quite literally their own and there's no boss to make sure they clock up the hours. Others have been surprised to realise that they're actually more productive than ever under such unrestrictive conditions. Anyone who dreams of being a travel writer will imagine the sense of liberation that comes with the ability to work not only from home, but from anywhere in the world.

Some of the most celebrated travel writers were famously obsessive about their office environment and effectively turned their backs on the essence of freedom that is one of the great compensations for such an uncertain and challenging career.

Tireless traveller Bruce Chatwin claimed he could only write at home, surrounded by his books. (And, in fact, he wrote only in a very rare type of notebook – now famous as Moleskine – that he bought in a small Parisian stationery store.) Paul Theroux, meanwhile, only uses a specific brand of ballpoint pen.

Truman Capote apparently only wrote when lying down and Joan Didion took this somnambulant obsession a step further by sleeping in her library so that she could get closer to her books. PG Wodehouse was so terrified of being disturbed that he wrote on a rowing boat that was anchored in the moat of his Norfolk retreat, Hunstanton Hall.

Even these examples pale to insignificance when compared to the extremes that Marcel Proust went to in his search for absolute peace: a cork-walled sound-proofed room was apparently still too raucous, so he bought up the neighbouring apartments and kept them empty as an inviolable barricade against noise.

Convincing yourself that your muse will elude you unless you're in predictable and reliable surroundings is like believing that the tooth fairy won't find you if you move house. Unable to work unless surrounded by familiarity, countless great writers brainwashed themselves out of the sheer sense of privileged freedom that comes from being able to work while on the road.

Paul Theroux wrote (in the typically excellent *Ghost Train to the Eastern Star*) about invitations to write articles while travelling: 'My Tao of Travel stipulates that such requests should be refused,' he said. 'Concentrate on where you are; do no back-home business; take no assignments; remain incommunicado; be scarce… keep your mind in the country you're in. That's the theory.'

It was doubtless a highly productive strategy for that particular trip since it appears that Theroux actually wrote the book during the return rail-journey to Asia, finishing it on the day he arrived home in London. While Theroux discourages writing about other places while travelling, it is interesting to note that he places no such restriction upon immersing himself in reading about other areas. His travel books are invariably dotted with reflections on the books he reads as he roams.

The problem with refusing to work while on the road is that it will vastly limit your writing time and potential. It's crucial to meet your deadlines – and quite often you might need to submit copy long before you've had a chance to settle into your favourite hometown café or to turn on the desk lamp in your study.

If you want to be a freelance travel writer then it will be hugely beneficial to train yourself to write from anywhere. Turn yourself into a sort of literary hobo. Embrace the thrill (and the challenge) of describing the hidden alleyways of Marrakech's souk while sitting in a teashop in Kuala Lumpur. Enjoy the privilege of being able to write while swinging in a hammock on the communal walkway of a Sarawak longhouse, or sitting cross-legged in a stilted hut on the Gambia River.

Been there, says Mark...

I consider it an inestimable privilege that I've been able to write from jungle camps, lodges, luxury hotels and backpacker flophouses all over the world, from Australia to Zimbabwe and from Argentina to Zanzibar. Making sure I get the writing done while still on the road has meant that I've often written with material still fresh in my mind and, just as important, I've been able to travel for longer spells. The increased level of familiarity to be had from actually living in a place (even for just a few weeks) enhances your understanding of a destination to a level that is beyond that of the typical fly-by-night tourist... and often beyond that of even the most inquisitive short-stay correspondents.

A career in travel writing is certainly not for everyone, but those who are determined to make it work are likely to find a greater level of freedom than would be possible in almost any other job. You need to approach this career with a professional outlook but if you have a deadline for an article on Paris and you plan to type it while lying beside a pool in Acapulco with a margarita in one hand... well, there's nobody who's going to stop you.

Been there, says Narina...

We all have different rhythms of working and while I agree it's important that, as a travel writer, one should be able to work from almost anywhere, actually writing from almost anywhere is something I struggle with. I'm easily distracted.

We're often away on assignment for weeks at a time, and those days are usually an irregular jumble of time spent in planes and taxis, exploring new places, meeting with people, moving from one hotel to another, researching areas of a city, heading out to photograph something specific, and spending hours or days with a guide. Finding both the space and time to sit down and write (uninterrupted) while we're on assignment can be challenging.

I try to manage my time wisely by doing the tasks that require shorter bouts of concentration – things like pitching, responding to emails, catching up on admin, working on photos – on the days when I'll have only an hour here and there to sit at my computer. When there is a deadline on the horizon, I'll try to keep a chunk of time clear so that I can sit down in our hotel room for at least three hours (offline) and dive into the feature.

It's a catch-22 because if I'm on assignment then it's a shame to be sitting behind my computer, but a few uninterrupted computer sessions are invaluable – for me, anyway – when it comes to getting the bones of the feature together. In order for this travel writing career to be sustainable, it's imperative to find a travelling / writing / admin balance that works for you.

THE EQUIPMENT YOU'LL NEED TO WORK REMOTELY

Narina swears by travelling with two notebooks – one for taking assignment notes and the other as a to-do list / organiser / planner / doodle book. I consider travelling with a hammock – one I designed years ago for an expedition – to be a wise move. We met a food writer once who never travels without his grinder of Himalayan salt. Different strokes for different folks.

While what you pack often comes down to personal preference, the list below details the things that I consider essential for travel writers.

ELECTRONICS WITH GOOD BATTERY LIFE

A laptop with a long battery life maximises your working hours and your freedom to work even where you can't find a power-source. I appreciate the space- and weight-saving benefits that come with using a 13-inch laptop. I'm a fan of Dell 2-in-1 laptops since they have a conveniently time-saving touchscreen function and they fold over to form a tablet, making them convenient for use on planes where elbowroom seems to reduce with each passing year.

A DUAL-SIM PHONE

Avoid the unwelcome surprise of hefty post-trip phone-bills by purchasing a pre-paid international travellers' SIM card. The one I use apparently works in 186 countries (I've yet to test it in all of them). A phone with dual-SIM is also a huge bonus and even more cost-effective since you can then buy local SIMs to use in each country while still keeping your international number active. Don't be a slave to cafes and hotels with Wi-Fi access – just use the local SIM to create a hotspot from your phone so that you'll have an Internet connection wherever you go.

BACKUP OPTIONS

It pays to be paranoid. I have a 256GB Micro SD card slotted into my computer – it's waterproof and shockproof so even if my laptop crashes or gets swamped (or even run over by a truck) I can simply remove the card to save my work. I backup to the Cloud but I also travel with a 1TB hard drive, which I carry in a separate bag from my computer.

Did I mention that I'm obsessive about backing up? So… I also have two other hard drives that are left at homes in the UK and Bali and could, as a last resort, be couriered to me without delay.

SUPPLEMENTARY POWER SOURCES

To work from the road, you're likely to need an impressive array of gadgets and you won't be able to work too far off the beaten track unless you have a plan to keep them all charged.

The smallest portable solar chargers are roughly the same size and weight as a smartphone and are useful when hiking as they can be attached to the top of your pack. They're useful for road-tripping too, but a better option is an inverter that plugs into the car's cigarette lighter. Rather than merely having the usual USB outlets of a standard cigarette-lighter adaptor, these inverters also allow you to charge a laptop, camera battery charger and other gadgets that normally plug into mains sockets.

A CAMERA YOU KNOW HOW TO USE

This book is not about photography, but there are major benefits for any freelance travel writer who takes the time to shoot as well as write (see chapter 11). If you intend to supply the images to illustrate your features, you'll need a good camera. A high-resolution point-and-shoot is the bare minimum, or a professional digital SLR if you intend to 'aim high'. I travel with a digital Nikon SLR (occasionally two bodies), three lenses and several 32GB memory cards. Even during a long assignment RAW images can be backed-up in four places: the cards; the laptop; the hard-drive; the Cloud. There's no excuse these days for losing your work. Ever.

THE FUTURE OF TRAVEL WRITING:
ARE WE ENTERING A NEW GOLDEN AGE?

The past decade has seen a marked decline in print publications and – precipitated by the Covid-19 pandemic – some of the biggest names have disappeared. At the same time there had, over the course of recent years, been a marked 'dumbing down' of online copy with editorial aiming at a readership that was assumed to have apparently a very limited intellect. Blocks of text more than five sentences long were often considered to be…

…beyond the concentration span of the average reader.

Algorithms and search engine optimisation – geared

towards the all-important ends of getting onto the first page of search engines – dictated the style of writing. Readability was often considered secondary. Writers were routinely asked to carve the copy into sections with subheads and bullet-points, making it extremely difficult to maintain a flowing narrative and catch the reader's imagination. It was a self-fulfilling prophesy since, faced with such infantile blurb, even the most devoted readers found their concentration levels lapsing still more.

Some writers prematurely mourned the 'death of print'. Many print publications folded entirely (no pun intended) or concentrated only on their online presence, with their contributor payrates plummeting. Inflight magazines – traditionally some of the best payers for freelancers – were hardest hit. In late 2019 I was working on a fairly regular basis for about a dozen inflight magazines (some of which occasionally paid over US$4,000 for a 1,500-word feature with photos). A year later only one was still printing and they were trying to stay alive by buying previously published articles.

But there is also some good news. Some of the best publications have reacted against the 'listicle' trend and are now deliberately commissioning more thoughtful, well-researched pieces. Some print magazines have switched to online publication only but, in a drive to maintain quality, have made a conscious decision to maintain their print rates for online copy. This trend could be the light at the end of the tunnel and the sign of a promising new era for travel writers. There's no reason why – with production costs substantially lowered in comparison to print – online publications shouldn't be able to match print payrates.

Well-crafted travel stories will always be in demand and – as readers begin to travel widely once again – online publications could manage a higher turnover of stories each month than they could ever do within the limitations of print. Editors will be able to respond more quickly to pitches and could have more leeway to accept offbeat stories. There will be less of a lead time before stories are published and, crucially for a freelance writer, payment is usually far prompter for websites than for magazines. The financial trauma of waiting five months or more for payment after an assignment (see chapter 9 for how finances work) could soon become a thing of the past.

§

3

HOW TO SET YOURSELF
UP AS A TRAVEL WRITER

by Mark Eveleigh

*It's none of their business that you
have to learn how to write. Let them
think you were born that way.*

– Ernest Hemingway –

Your first features will, in all likelihood, be the hardest to publish. There's no alternative to perseverance, however, and with some of the tips in this chapter you might be surprised at just how smoothly you can set yourself up as a published travel writer.

In 1975 American magazine writer Duane Newcomb wrote *A Complete Guide to Marketing Magazine Articles*. In the first sentence of the chapter entitled 'How to Sell Everything You Write' Newcomb pointed out that 'no matter how long you've been selling, you won't sell everything the first time out.' Five years later (in *The Travel Writer's Handbook*) Louise Purwin Zobel reported a conversation in which professional travel writers were discussing where to send a story first…and then, if that didn't lead to a sale, where they should send it next.

If you follow the steps outlined in chapter 5 on how to write the perfect pitch, there is no reason why you shouldn't get to the stage where you're producing around 40 features a year and billing for *every single one*. But before we get to that point there are some bridges to cross.

CHASING YOUR FIRST GIG

Whenever you approach an editor, do your best to come across like a seasoned veteran. There's no room for a hint of nervously faltering suggestion that the editor might, just maybe, think your idea has enough potential to commission you. You should be so enthusiastic about the idea you're pitching that the editor will find it irresistible.

Most editors who commission a unpublished writer will probably stipulate that if the story submitted isn't up to scratch, it won't be published and you won't be paid. In effect, this is pretty much the same situation that you'll face right throughout your career. As an experienced writer with a hefty portfolio of published stories, you should usually be able to demand a 50% 'kill fee' (see chapter 9) if, through no fault of yours, a story gets rejected. If one of your stories is rejected because the copy was substandard, however, you will almost certainly lose this client.

Harsh fact: no matter how established you become as a freelancer you're only ever as good as the last story you wrote.

Been there, says Narina...

When I was working full-time as an editor, I'd regularly receive emails from people who'd never been published but wanted to 'write for magazines'. Many would send me examples of their writing (often on topics and in styles that didn't relate to the publication I edited) and ask vaguely if there was anything that they could write for me. Not a great way to try to get a foot in the door.

A far better approach is to pitch an editor with specific ideas that are relevant to the title they're working on. To show off your writing ability, attach as a sample something you've written (around 500 to 800 words) that you believe would fit well in the magazine you're approaching. The fact that you haven't been published before becomes less important if you can show the editor that you're able to write something that is worth reading.

As a side note, if I was approached by someone who had been published only once or twice then I always asked to receive their writing examples as Word documents rather than a PDF of their published work. A PDF of the magazine pages might look better (and be proof that the writer had been published), but an editor might have worked extensively to improve that copy and therefore it wouldn't be a true reflection of the writer's abilities.

WRITING FOR 'EXPOSURE'

Whenever you get tempted to write for 'exposure' remind yourself that people die of exposure.

Most people who are starting out in the freelance writing business seem to think that there's no alternative to working for free in the early days. In my opinion, this is completely wrong. Few editors are so naïve that they don't recognise which publications are the non-payers. Such publications are therefore reserved solely for amateurs and an entire portfolio of published features in titles like this will only serve to demonstrate your lack of faith in the worth of your own work. 'Sure, none of these people paid me,' you're implying each time you pitch, 'but I'm hoping that this time it might be different.'

If the mood hits you, inspiration strikes and you have the makings of a story bubbling over so that it just has to be written without a moment's delay, then by all means put it on your own website or your blog. The chance of selling an article that has already been published like this is slim, but it's not impossible.

Been there, says Mark...

For the first decade of my career as a writer my golden rule was to never write for free. Ever. Under any circumstances.

Then, about 10 years ago Narina and I started working on a blog together. Sure, we'd hoped we would make money from it eventually, but long before that started to happen I realised what incredible freedom there was in being able to write about absolutely anything that fascinated me. It was a breath of fresh air amid the steady run of magazine deadlines and I still look back upon those unpaid workdays as some of the most enjoyable writing stints of my career.

Furthermore, I enjoyed it so much and got snatched up on the blogging wave to such an extent that on several occasions I bent my own rule and also wrote for other high-profile sites and blogs for free (Huffpost etc) in return for exchanged links. Somehow, even then, I still kept it quiet as if it was some sort of shameful secret. Like a lame gazelle under the watchful eyes of a hyaena, I hid this sign of my weakness from editors.

If you want to get into print as a professional writer then it stands to reason that there is really no way to do so other than the professional way. But if you feel that your work is best suited to online publications, then there are many prestigious sites that pay quite well – and, frequently far more promptly than print publications. Some relatively healthy payers I've written for from time to time have been the BBC Travel, CNN Travel and National Geographic websites.

A GOLDEN NUGGET OF ADVICE
FOR AN AMBITIOUS ROOKIE

If you want to write something worth reading then first do something worth writing about. If you are really determined to get noticed, then set out to do something so stunningly unique that editors are simply not going to be able to overlook you.

It's not necessary that your experience be an absolute world-first or a trailblazing expedition. Just decide on something that fascinates you and for which you have particular enthusiasm; you might want to hunt down the best espresso in Italy, learn kickboxing in Thailand, travel the length of India by rail or herd guineapigs in Ecuador.

Once you've completed a suitably fascinating trip and can demonstrate that you have sufficient material for a unique travel feature, you stand an excellent chance of being commissioned to write it. This is assuming you have the skills to put together a professional pitch (see chapter 5).

Been there, says Mark...

In 1995 I applied for a travel bursary and was sponsored (by Heineken) to lead an expedition into Central Borneo. In line with Heineken's marketing slogan, I was tasked with 'reaching the parts that other explorers had not yet reached'.

The expedition was fraught with disaster almost from the outset and we (barely) survived everything from shipwreck to dysentery, barbecued mousedeer foetus, and malaria. For a writer, however, there's no such thing as bad experiences. There's just good material. I realised that if I couldn't write a book about that trip, I'd never be able to write anything.

I was offered an advance by a publisher and found a room in Madrid's old town where I hammered the manuscript out between shivering bouts of that same recurring malaria. That first book (which shall remain nameless since it embarrasses me these days as the work of a rookie) was far from a best-seller. Nevertheless, it garnered some positive reviews and gave me the first small touch of notoriety that brought me to the notice of a few magazine editors.

§

4

INSIGHT INTO HOW MAGAZINES WORK

by Narina Exelby

*A professional writer is an amateur
who didn't quit.*

— Richard Bach —

You're reading this book because you want to be a *freelance travel writer*, not someone who's tied to an office job... so why on earth is there a chapter here about how editorial teams are structured, and what goes on in magazine offices? Because *you want to be a freelance travel writer* – and it is the people on those editorial teams who will commission you to write those stories, and it is they who will work with your words and send them out into the world.

'Magazine Land' has to be one of the most curious places on earth. Mystical to those who've never visited, it's often elevated to glamorous heights by those who worship its glossy pages – and yet in reality, it's often cranky, crazy, untidy and sometimes very small and dusty. It is, however, a wonderful place crafted on caffeine, keyboards and late nights, by people with fast fingers, wild imaginations and an insatiable curiosity.

It is a place of passion, frustration and ecstasy. Littered with press releases, desktops are often consumed by books; drawers are cluttered with products sent by hopeful PR companies; and there are piles of dated magazines to which the makers are too emotionally attached to recycle. It is a place that is always – always – ruled by deadlines.

Eagle-eyes are usually a prerequisite for entry and things like where to put a comma and finding the precise words for a caption are infinitely important. It can – and often does – take days to choose the correct words to grace a cover. Finding the right photograph? Weeks. Months sometimes. But what makes 'Magazine Land' particularly strange is that it exists in a time-warp. Your diary says it's February? Mag-Land's living in April. In fact, in some parts, your next summer has already come and gone.

After living and breathing magazines for more than 13 years, these quirks became my normal. I never gave words like flatplan, spread, wobbler, blow-in, blurb or bucket a second thought until a few months before I went freelance, when an intern's forehead crinkled in utter confusion when I set out to explain how things worked. As I took her on The Grand Tour of our magazine's production cycle, I was reminded that (as far as I was aware) there is no comprehensive guidebook to working in magazines and that getting in and getting around can be daunting.

This book has been written to help you get travel features published in magazines, and so this chapter will focus on the magazine process – but keep in mind that many digital publications and print newspapers will work in a similar way.

HOW PUBLICATIONS MAKE MONEY – AND WHY IS THIS RELEVANT TO YOU, THE FREELANCE WRITER

In the simplest terms, there are two departments involved in the production of a magazine: editorial and advertising. The editorial team will take care of the editorial pages (those that are listed on the contents page), and the ad-sales team sells advertising space. Income generated from advertising is what pays salaries and keeps the business afloat, while income from the sale of the magazine, in comparison, tends to be rather small.

As a writer, it's important to keep this in mind because while editorial teams usually take pride in being independent, the bills are paid by the ad-sales team and so it's really important to them that the advertisers are happy with the editorial content that is produced. In every publication I've worked on there has been a love-hate relationship between editorial and advertising teams as we've tried to navigate the fine line between maintaining editorial integrity and keeping the advertisers happy.

If you're a freelance writer, it's well worth flipping through a magazine (print or digital) and getting to know who the major advertisers are, because pitching features that are in alignment with who advertises in the title could well swing an editor's decision to commission your feature over another. If, for example, many advertisers have products or properties based in Spain then there's a good chance the editor might be interested in a feature from that country.

WHO DOES WHAT – AND WHY IT'S IMPORTANT THAT YOU KNOW THIS

It's good to understand how the editorial team is structured so that you know who to contact when you're sending through pitches – but please do keep in mind that what follows here is a very general and simple overview. Over the past 15 years particularly, most editorial teams have shrunk to the point where people now fill multiple positions and these days very few media companies have the luxury of what was once a full editorial team.

The structure of an editorial team will usually be as follows: editor-in-chief, editor, art director, deputy editor, managing editor, sub-editor, section editors, picture editor, designers and writers.

Ultimately everyone will report to the editor-in-chief who steers the editorial direction of the title. The editor takes charge of the content and oversees the rest of the editorial team. On some titles, the editor will commission freelancers, but often this is left to the section editors, who focus on a particular aspect of the magazine (see magazine structure, in the next section). The managing editor drives the production process, and it is the sub-editor who gets the content into shape (making sure each piece has a headline and blurb, that the content is grammatically and factually correct, and that it's the right length). The art director is responsible for the design of the title; the picture editor sources images and the designers work their magic to weave words and images together.

Editors often have a list of their favourite contributors and freelancers. These will be writers and photographers who have skills in particular areas (for example, they're good at doing interviews, or creating a sense of place, or tackling scientific stories); the editors will know that they can rely on these freelancers to deliver quality copy – on time. Work on developing a good relationship with an editor, and chances are you'll be top of their mind when a relevant story needs writing or shooting.

THE STRUCTURE OF A MAGAZINE – AND HOW TO USE THIS TO YOUR ADVANTAGE

A standard piece of advice for freelance writers is to familiarise yourself with the magazine before you send through any pitches. Many freelancers interpret this as 'read one or two stories to see what the tone is' – but if you take time to get to grips with how a magazine is structured then you will be able to craft pitches that are very relevant to that specific title, in a way that appeals to the editors. And that, of course, increases the chances of your pitch being accepted. (See chapter 5 for more on pitching.)

No matter what they cover, most magazines have a similar structure. There'll be the front-of-book section, the features well, and the back-of-book section. Running through these sections will be the content pillars (sometimes called 'buckets'), and these vary from title to title. Here's what these sections are all about, and what you need to look out for:

THE FRONT OF BOOK

First up in a magazine are the regulars and the bitsy pages: the editor's letter, the contents pages, and the snippets and news sections. These are usually put together in-house, and the snippets and news will often be compiled by a junior member of the team. A lot of this content will be adapted from press releases that have been sent in, and stem from desk-based research by said junior.

There's not much room here for freelance travel writers, but if you're wanting to secure some regular work (which is a real gift for freelancers) then pay attention to these pages because this is a great place for you to carve yourself a niche. If you're always up to speed with new developments in the tourism industry, then perhaps you could pitch yourself as the best person to write the monthly 'hot new openings' page; or if you're a bookworm who has great connections in a variety of publishing houses then you might like to offer book reviews of upcoming releases.

If you're just starting out as a travel writer, contributing to these up-front pages can be a really great way to get your foot in the door and earn a small steady income at the same time.

THE FEATURES WELL

This, of course, is what you're aiming for: it's the main section of the publication and is where longer stories – usually between 800 and 2,000 words – are run.

When you're looking through a magazine, take note of how the features are structured: does the story run in one unbroken length of text, or is it divided by subheads? Are the features first-person narratives, or travel guides, or roundups? Does the feature include sidebars or boxes of text that tie in with the main body of the story? Is there a 'planner' or 'fact-file' page where practical details such as getting around and where to stay are included? Use this knowledge when you're putting your pitch together.

THE BACK OF BOOK

This small section is often where regular columns (usually one-pagers) are placed, and sometimes a few bitsy pages like supplier details or listings. Take a look through a few issues of the same title – if a column is written by a different person each month, it could be worth pitching something for this space. If you have an idea for a regular column, pitch that too – who knows, the editor might well be looking for someone new to fill that space.

THE CONTENT PILLARS

Content pillars are the themes on which the magazine's content is based. In a travel title the content pillars could include adventure, culture, food, wellness, inspiration, luxury travel, destination guides and so on. It's the mix of these that makes each travel publication different.

Sometimes the pillars are obvious and the words 'Adventure' or 'Wellness', for example, are written in the top strap (the very top part of the page); sometimes they're not shown at all, but the editor keeps them top of mind when planning each issue. If you're having difficulty figuring out what they are, click onto the publication's website – the pillars are often used to organize the website's menu bar.

What's the point of identifying a publication's content pillars? Well, an obvious reason is that you'll be wasting your time if you pitch a hardcore adventure story to a magazine whose pillars are luxury, wellness and city breaks. Another reason is that you can send one editor a variety of pitches (from the same trip) that tie in with the different content pillars, and therefore you maximise your chances of having a feature from that trip published in that magazine.

Let's say you've spent a week eating your way around Bangkok. Instead of sending through a generic 'street food in Bangkok' pitch, you've done your homework and know that the magazine's content pillars are People, Travel Guides, Food, Adventure – and so you pitch the following: a story based on some of the characters of Bangkok's street-food scene (People); five must-visit night markets in Bangkok (Travel Guide); an in-depth piece on the one ingredient Thai chefs swear by (Food); the quest to eat the strangest snacks sold in Bangkok's markets (Adventure).

EDITORIAL THEMES AND LINE-UPS

Some publications choose to theme their issues; if they do so then the majority of the content is likely to nod to the theme in some way. While most editors keep the details of their editorial line-ups a closely guarded secret, some might be willing to let you know what themes they have planned for the next few issues. Ask if they give these out – it will help you to put together relevant pitches.

With every issue they create, editorial teams will work off a line-up, which is a document that outlines the structure and the content of the magazine, as well as how many pages a particular section and piece of content has been given. Keep in mind that when they commission stories, editors know how many pages they have been assigned to – and they know how many words their magazine runs per page (the word count will vary according to the page's position within the structure). You won't be paid for the extra words you write, so don't waste your time.

THE TIMELINE OF A MAGAZINE CYCLE

Monthly magazines usually work two or three months in advance. Let's say, for example, that the month we're in right now is October. This means that a monthly magazine's editorial team will be working on the pages of the December issue, which will go to print at the end of this month (October). At the same time, the team will be receiving, writing and editing copy for the January issue, and commissioning copy for the February issue. Next month (in November), the team will be working on the January pages, receiving, writing and editing content for the February issue, and commissioning the March issue. So at any one time, the editorial team is working usually two months ahead, and on three different issues.

It's important to keep this in mind when you do your own pitching and travel planning (particularly if you're targeting print publications) because if you want to write a story on the Christmas markets in Madrid, for example, you'll need to submit your copy in September. An editor might want to run a story with a distinct summer focus in the late spring, and so they'd need to receive the copy in late winter. Get the picture? The bottom line is, if you're wanting to write a feature that is time-specific and you'll be pitching a print publication, you're going to need to pitch far in advance.

Been there, says Narina...

Back when I worked full-time on a travel magazine, I popped into a supermarket to buy some cheese. We were nearing the end of deadline week, which meant that my days had been consumed with proofreading (multiple times) all of the editorial pages that would soon be sent to print. We were wrapping up the December issue, so I'd spent the week intensively reading and re-reading about festive-season holidays and bucket-list travel destinations for the new year. Also, I'd been checking that the very basics of the pages – the issue date and page numbers – were correct. So, December was totally on my mind.

Anyway, there I was in the dairy aisle looking for a block of cheddar when I realised that the cheese I'd just picked up had passed its sell-by date. I picked up another one, then another – and soon realised that all of the cheddar had expired. Outrageous! I'm an easy-going person who does their best to avoid conflict, but this deadline had been particularly stressful and right there, in the dairy aisle, something in me snapped.

'Excuse me,' I said quite loudly to the man restocking the milk shelves, 'all this cheese has passed its sell-by date. I need to speak to the manager.'

The man looked at the cheese in my hand and very

politely told me it was fine.

'Uh, no it's not. This is unacceptable,' I insisted as other shoppers started to stare. 'I must speak to the manager.'

The man picked up another block of cheddar and showed me the expiry date. 'It says best before 10 November,' he pointed out gently.

'Exactly!' I snapped. '10 November – and it's now Decem....'

The penny dropped. It was October; my mind was lost in magazine time. I muttered an apology, ran from the store, and have not returned since.

§

5

HOW TO PITCH STORIES THAT EDITORS WANT

by Mark Eveleigh

The most essential gift for a good writer is a built-in shock-proof shit detector.

– Ernest Hemingway –

I know freelance writers who detest pitching stories, but my philosophy is to look upon this process as part of the initial inspiration for the sort of dream trips that are the delightful bread-and-butter of a travel writer's working life. It's almost impossible to make a living from this business if you don't actively enjoy the challenge of pitching. Striving for pitch-perfection is a vital part of the craft for any freelance writer.

Been there, says Narina...

Back in the years when I worked full-time editing magazines, I'd regularly receive emails from people who wanted to write for us. Many were just starting out on their writing careers and so this might have come down to their lack of experience, but so often I was surprised by how badly constructed, incorrect or inappropriate their emails and pitches were.

The following snippets of advice address some of the most common issues I came across:

Send your pitch to the correct person

A look at the publication's website, a simple phone call or email to the magazine's enquiry line should clear this up.

Make sure you're emailing the correct person at the correct publication

I'd often receive emails from people who'd cut and pasted the story idea they sent to a competing title, and then forgotten to change the editor or the magazine's name. Not a good first impression – at all.

Keep your abbreviations and emojis for your friends

And spell-check your email.

Be familiar with the title you're pitching

Know what type of stories they run, what destinations

they cover, what structure their stories tend to follow, who their audience is and know the tone of the magazine. This is very important – it shows you understand the mag and will be able to deliver a piece that's on-brand.

Do some research

Look specifically at issues published within the past year. It's unlikely the editor will accept a story if they've just run a similar feature on the same destination or topic.

Work your angle

Do your best to find an angle that is interesting, relevant to the magazine, that's unlikely to have been covered before and that is unlikely to be covered by competing titles.

Be up front about your sponsors

Be open about who's covering the costs of your trip. If it's sponsored by a company, they'll want exposure in your story – and the magazine's policy might not allow this. See chapter 10 for more on this.

Be specific

Tell the editor what they can expect from you and what your strengths and interests are. 'I'm a certified diver and a qualified marine biologist, so I'll be able to write with authority about the Great Barrier Reef.' 'My French is fluent and I plan on talking to many locals in the food markets of Marrakech, finding out first-hand the secret to cooking the perfect tagine.'

Attach one or two examples of your work

If the editor can see you write well but your pitch doesn't fit the magazine, they'll be more likely to work with you to find an angle that suits their brand.

Follow up

Don't bombard the editor with phone calls and emails, but if you've not heard from them after two weeks, drop them a polite reminder – chances are that deadlines have taken over and your email's gotten lost in the mayhem of their inbox. It happens. Honest.

SEND A PITCH, OR SEND A STORY?

'Where's your favourite place in the world? It's the first question people ask. They quickly follow this up with: 'So, how does it work? Do magazines send you to places, or do you write stories and then try to sell them…?'

As an incorrigible nomad, I don't have a satisfactory answer to the first question. I'm lucky enough, after all, to be able to travel regularly between places I love. On the second question, however, I am 100% decisive: I *never* write a story without a confirmed commission upfront.

It always astounds me when I hear experienced writers explain that they often write the story first and then try to sell it 'on-spec'.

I've never once written a piece without knowing ahead of time that a specific editor is committed to using it. In my experience it's best to pitch first because every publication has a different readership and the ideal wordcount, style, format and slant (the specific angle that will most appeal to that readership) are rarely the same.

Many editors will assume that an existing story may have already been rejected by one or more of their competitors. (Some editors will reject a perfectly good story rather than face the potential embarrassment of accepting something that was rejected by a competing editor.) It's also possible that an editor will like the general idea behind your pitch, but will ask for the story to focus on one specific aspect.

Been there, says Mark...

A couple of years ago I was commissioned by National Geographic Traveler *to do a tongue-in-cheek 'baptism of fire' story on the art of the South African braai (barbecue). Unfortunately, the magazine closed the month before my story was due to run. In line with the organisation's reputation, I was nevertheless paid in full. I was left, however, with an article that I had worked hard to complete.*

I did my best to resell it but had almost given up in my efforts when, two years later, the editor of a UK travel magazine agreed to run it. It was at a wildly reduced rate (but then I had already been well paid once, after all). The difficulty in getting that 'on-spec' story published seemed to confirm my opinion that trying to sell something you've already written is rarely fruitful. On the other hand, the UK-based editor so appreciated the style of the piece that he suggested I produce a regular column along similar lines for the front-of-book section of the magazine. So, apparently, submitting on-spec can work out well from time-to-time.

IS IT BEST TO PITCH BEFORE YOU GO ON A TRIP, OR ONCE YOU RETURN?

Unless you have a proven track-record and a portfolio of published articles it will usually be preferable to pitch once your trip is complete. The editor is going to have to gamble on your talents and ability to get the thing written and it may well be taking things a step too far for them to rely on the fact that your trip will be as exciting as you planned. Even the most experienced pitch-writer will admit that 'you won't believe what I've just experienced' is a more persuasive tone to take than 'this is what I hope to do…'.

Been there, says Narina…

I tend to pitch both before and after a trip. Having at least one confirmed commission before we travel helps me to plan the trip, know where to focus my attention, and I can be sure to get the material needed.

Almost always we'll come across unexpected angles or story leads when we travel, and so I'd pitch these angles afterwards – particularly if something interesting pops up that I know would be perfect for a particular title.

A good example of this would be a trip I did to Botswana, where I was reviewing some safari camps for The Telegraph. *While at one of the camps I met the Zimbabwean owner of the safari company and realised what a brilliant 'take my advice' piece his journey would make for* Men's Health. *The editor confirmed that commission, and the feature was an absolute gift to write.*

HOW TO CRAFT THE IDEAL PITCH

Writing a good pitch takes just as much talent as writing the story itself. Arguably it might take even more since you're more tightly confined into a wordcount of, ideally, under 100 words. Yet putting together an appealing pitch is crucial if you expect to get an invitation to write and get paid for the feature.

Spend at least as much time polishing your pitch as you'd spend polishing the finished feature. An editor is unlikely to have faith in the professionalism of a writer who sends through a pitch containing spelling mistakes or grammatical or factual errors.

Use the following guidelines to put your pitch email together:

INCLUDE YOUR PERSONAL BIO

In as few words as possible, give your writing background and credentials, showing why you will be the perfect new writer for the publication. (This is aimed at convincing editors to commission you for one of the pitches to follow in this same email, and also to instil the idea that this might be the start of an ongoing working relationship).

If you've had features published already then attach them or, because some editors won't open files from unknown sources, upload them to your website or to an online portfolio such as www.clippings.me. If you haven't had anything published yet don't feel disheartened – this is the section of the pitching email in which to sing up any other skills (languages or travel experience) that are relevant to the regions you're going to be pitching stories from.

INTRODUCE THE PITCHES

To have the best chance of catching your dinner you might want to fish with a throw-net rather than with a single hook. My ideal pitching email would include three or four very different ideas and angles from a variety of destinations.

Each pitch must potentially fit with the style of the magazine, but don't be shy about thinking a little out of the box. You never know what was discussed in the latest editorial meeting and perhaps there was a suggestion of some changes of tack if editors / publishers / sales team consider they are getting stuck in a rut with content.

You should already be aware of the style of the magazine so you can hope that any of these pitches might appeal – at the very least this indication of imagination and enthusiasm will show the editor that you are a contributor who is able to come up with suggestions. It's not unusual that instead of accepting one of your pitches, the editor will appreciate your versatility and suggest instead that you write a feature with a completely different angle.

Apologise for swamping the editor with ideas and promise to 'keep the following pitches as brief as possible', adding that 'if more details are required don't hesitate to let me know'.

THE PITCHES

Try to restrict each pitch to around 100 words and give each one a bold heading so that the editor can scan through and ignore any of the story ideas that lack instant appeal.

A pitch should be a condensed version of the article you hope to write and, just as you'd hope to snag a reader's interest with your first line, you must do so with the pitch, too. Mention the location, the subject and any sources or experts who might be central to the story.

INCLUDE SUBJECT AND DESTINATION

Be certain that you are pitching regions that the publication covers, and if they cover diverse stories from all over the globe then feel free to rack your brains for ideas that they're unlikely to have touched on before.

For a global magazine with a wide scope of interests I might pitch a feature on a horse-riding safari in South Africa; Bangkok's finest secret street-food venues; a conservation story from a research project in the Amazon; and a story on literary hangouts in Madrid. Clearly as time goes by, a travel writer has opportunities to collect a wider variety of potential stories but don't be shy about mixing pitches from trips you've already made with pitches for assignments you'd *like to do*.

CRAFT YOUR SIGN-OFF

Throw in a quick apology for the fact that the pitches have (as they invariably do) extended longer than you'd expected… but blame it on your enthusiasm and the 'wide scope of potential material'.

End the email with a polite sign-off expressing your enthusiasm for establishing an ongoing working relationship and perhaps include a sneaky mention of 'upcoming trips that are looming on the horizon'. These trips – effectively mini-pitches that help to spread your net still wider – might actually be planned or might just be places you'd like to go if you had a commission. It's not unusual to have the pitches in your email rejected for one reason or another, but to receive an invitation to send other pitches for one of these 'planned' trips.

If an editor gives the green light for one of your pitches on a destination you haven't visited yet, they will usually be flexible enough about the deadline to give you time to pull it together. You need to be sure in advance that you can afford the outlay of the trip, so it's wise to restrict such pitches to locations that are either close to home or relatively inexpensive to access. Jack's Flight Club (www.jacksflightclub.com) is an excellent starting place for looking for inexpensive flights. A pro account is a worthwhile investment for any traveller since it gives you earliest access to the best deals and, often irresistible, 'error prices' where airlines accidentally advertise ridiculously cheap flights.

Every established freelance travel writer is likely to have their own pitch format, but the above is my preferred pitch scenario for an editor I've not yet written for. The more established the working relationship becomes, the more freedom you have to drop quick messages along the lines of 'Hey mate – just came across an idea that might appeal…'.

POST-PITCH PATIENCE

How long should you wait for an editor to reply before you move on and pitch someone else? Unfortunately, there's no concrete answer to this question. Some editors are notoriously slow at replying, while even the relatively prompt repliers can let several weeks pass before they look at the pitches they've received, or get around to commissioning forthcoming issues.

Be extremely cautious, however, of falling into the trap where you pitch two similar stories to competing titles. If the editors commission you to write the features and both stories go to print in simultaneous issues, you're likely to find yourself black-listed from *both* publications in the future.

To avoid this, try to make sure that articles you pitch could be given a wildly different slant – ideally sufficiently different so that a reader could scarcely recognise the same subject matter.

REJECTED PITCHES

Hopefully your pitch will meet an enthusiastic reception and will be perfectly timed so that you'll be rewarded with a swift and positive response. Freelance travel writing is often a numbers game, so don't be despondent if you get a rejection or, more often, no reply whatsoever. This happens even to the most established freelancer. There can be a variety of reasons why perfectly good pitches don't get accepted even when they come from a magazine's regular contributors.

Often these reasons are beyond the control of even the most experienced pro:

• The subject or topic might have been covered in a recent (or forthcoming) issue. If this turns out to be the case, then take encouragement from the fact that at least you're hitting upon the right kind of ideas.

• The editor might already have features lined up that cover the region you're pitching. Wait a couple of weeks so that the editor doesn't think you're hassling and then try pitches from other areas.

• Sometimes it's a question of marketing and advertising revenue. Your ground-breaking, earth-shattering Cambodia pitch might have been rejected simply because some favoured advertiser in the magazine has been promised a Thailand story in that issue.

Been there, says Narina...

It's not necessarily the end of the world if a publication rejects the story you've been commissioned to write.

Years ago, I wrote a travel feature that centred on shells. I'd worked exceptionally hard on the research side, photographed the feature extensively, and was very proud of what I'd produced. The editor said he was thrilled with the feature... but a few weeks later he emailed to say that they wouldn't be running the story. 'Our new publisher has stipulated that, with immediate effect, we are to stay away from nature-focussed content,' he wrote.

I was gutted and wallowed in self-pity for a while, convincing myself that the rejection was an indication of the quality of my work, rather than a change in the magazine's editorial direction. The fact that they paid me 100% of the agreed word rate helped to ease the blow.

A week later I contacted the editor of another magazine and asked if she'd be interested in the (already written) story. She requested a slight rewrite to bring it in line with her title – more travel, less science – and three months after it was rejected by one publisher, my shells story was the cover feature for British Airway's inflight magazine.

WILL AN EDITOR STEAL YOUR IDEA?

In quarter of a century of freelancing I've had a story idea purloined (not to say 'stolen') just once. I pitched a feature on Tangier (a city I knew very well at the time) to the inflight magazine of a major airline. The pitch was rejected but I was surprised to stumble across almost *exactly the same story* several months later in the magazine.

It seemed that my idea had been given to the celebrity writer John McCarthy. (I must admit that the title 'McCarthy's Bazaar' had a nice ring to it and – tying in as it did with the bestselling book *McCarthy's Bar* – I wondered if this might have been one of the reasons why he got the gig rather than me.) I didn't complain to the editor, however; in part because I hoped to maintain a good working relationship… and in part because McCarthy had spent five years as a hostage in Lebanon and probably deserved a fun trip if anyone did.

It was a rare case though, and I decided just to write it off to experience. In general, there's no point in searching out ideas for irresistible travel features if you're going to be too nervous to mention them to editors.

§

6

WHAT TO EXPECT FROM CONTRACTS AND AGREEMENTS

by Mark Eveleigh

When the going gets weird, the weird turn pro.

– Hunter S Thompson –

'Can you cover Sudan for us?'

These six words from the editor of Etihad Airline's inflight magazine (along with an emailed ticket) amounted to the only written 'contract' I had for what turned out to be a three-week assignment to Khartoum (in the thick of election riots) and a 2,000km road-trip to a remote section of the Sudanese Sahara.

While some editors will send a comprehensive commission form (which includes word count, pay rate, story details, invoicing details, stipulated kill fee etc), contracts are not always issued for travel writing assignments.

Most outsiders to this business would consider it utterly bizarre that freelancers routinely set off to remote parts of the world (usually at their own expense) at the merest nod from an editor. In almost any other industry a 50% deposit would be considered a bare minimum but, in lieu of that, you're not likely to see any financial recompense for at least a month or two after your feature has been published.

Some editors might not be prepared to commit to even a vague agreement upfront, and instead might suggest that they're potentially keen but would rather wait to hear an update once the trip has been completed. It's impossible to advise upon such a scenario since every pitch and every trip (including the expenses involved) differs. In effect the only thing you can do in such a scenario is to go with your gut feel. No editor is likely to resent it if you decide not to take the risk of running up expenses based on such a vague offer. On the other hand, you might feel confident that the trip is going to be a rich mine of material and that the editor will surely be convinced when you return. Just as importantly, there may also be other markets you could sell to at a later date.

In my book (and this *is* my book) the rare negative incidents where this easy-going attitude backfires are more than compensated for if a freelancer can garner a reputation for being pro-active and easy to work with.

Been there, says Mark...

I was halfway through a road-trip along South Africa's Garden Route when I heard that Kenyan Airways' inflight magazine – a regular client of mine – had closed and that the commission I'd been working on for the last week would have to be canned. Given the fact that the magazine's entire in-house staff were apparently now jobless, I didn't feel that I could complain too bitterly. So, I was pleasantly surprised when the publishers very decently honoured the typically vague (i.e., unwritten) agreement I had with the editor and paid me a 50% kill fee. I continued with the trip anyway and was subsequently able to sell stories to several other magazines.

COMMISSION FORMS GIVE YOU THE BASICS

Some editors habitually send out commission forms, which outline what they're expecting from you. Each publication will have its own format and style, but a commissioning form will generally include deadline date, word count, pay rate, and general story outline. You'll not need to sign this, but it's as close to a contract as you'll usually get.

For new clients, whose style and format you might not be familiar with, it's crucial to make sure you're on the same page as the editor (no pun intended). Ask to see two or three sample PDFs of stories that the editor considered hit just the right tone and style. (There are added benefits to this: you now have an insight into what standards you must live up to; and you know who your greatest freelance competitors are.)

Make sure too that you have a firm idea of the content and angle needed… but don't allow yourself to get so fixated that the story is already panning out around preconceived ideas even before you've arrived on location. Good editors are aware that the best stories often develop on the road and the most experienced of them will often agree with your changes of direction if you update mid-trip suggesting a fascinating about-turn that could transform a good feature into a *great* one.

Something to look out for on the commission form is whether a kill-fee is mentioned. Articles can get 'killed' (that's publishing-speak) for a variety of reasons, ranging from political unrest or natural disaster in the country you've written about, to the whims and fancies of a new editor. A kill-fee will stipulate what the writer will get paid should the feature not be published (for reasons that are no fault of their own). As a professional travel writer, it is your responsibility to ensure that you never have a situation where a story is rejected because the writing is sub-standard. Chapter 7 offers some tips on sidestepping that nastiest of journalistic pitfalls.

COMMISSIONING LETTERS
SHOW YOU'RE LEGIT

I have an instinctive intolerance for bureaucracy and believe that most busy editors appreciate a freelancer who'll take off and hit the road without the need for niggly pieces of paper... but there are times when a 'commissioning letter' can help to open doors, greasing the creaking hinges of bureaucracy.

A commissioning letter is especially handy on last-minute assignments where you'll be photographing for the feature and haven't had time to make prior contact with locations or venues (museums, exhibitions, tourist attractions). Such a letter will normally stipulate the content required for the article, and it is useful if it includes the readership figures, number of pages the story will have and an expected date of publication. This letter will establish your credentials and save on drawn-out explanations if time is so short that you arrive unannounced at a property or tourist venue.

In an era when hotels, PR companies and tour operators are being mobbed by influencers, a press card can also prove your credentials. You can apply for a press card through the International Travel Writers Alliance (www.internationaltravelwritersalliance.com), the world's largest association of professional travel journalists.

CORPORATE RED TAPE

Within the last decade or so some of the bigger publishing organisations (presumably those with their own phalanxes of lawyers) have introduced standard forms that have to be filled out by every contributor.

If you want to write for the *BBC Travel* website, for example, you're likely to have to fill in a 'writer agreement', an 'online commissioning agreement', a 'bank registration form' and a 'purchase order form'. For a short initial commission, it can sometimes seem that your time is more tied up filling in the forms than actually writing the feature. Fortunately, you don't have to fill these out for every subsequent commission because you'll be registered permanently in the system for ongoing work. There's a benefit often in this system since payment may be issued automatically without the need for you to file invoices for each job.

When contracts do exist, there will normally be little scope for changes to be made. Normally they are simply standard forms stipulating what the obligations are for both parties, what the fees are and what rights are offered, what expenses are covered (normally *none*) and what the kill-fee is should the story be canned through no fault of the writer (usually 50%). They will also expect confirmation that the work has been produced solely by the writer, that 'the writer owns or controls all rights in the work (and all part(s) thereof)' and that it has not been published elsewhere.

Unfortunately, things often get more complex for the contributor when a contract is thrown into the equation. Contracts are normally designed, after all, to benefit the issuer of that contract rather than the person to whom it is directed. Likewise, in the case of contracts there's often little leeway in negotiating changes.

When an editor commissions you to write a story it's normally implied that you're giving away only the simple first rights for print publication (some might include mention of online use – see chapter 9 for a cautionary note on this). It seems that, almost invariably, when a contract is involved you're expected to give away more than that and your story will often run online with no extra payment.

SUBMIT A COMPREHENSIVE INVOICE

The most pleasant piece of paperwork you might ever have to complete could be the first invoice you write for a hefty figure, billed to a prestigious title. You might hope to write more than a few invoices over the years so it's worth starting out by creating a professional-looking template.

It doesn't hurt to have an invoice header that stands out from the reams of others. If you're a photographer you might want to create a banner with one of your most eye-catching images (I have my name and contact details as text across this banner). If you're purely a writer, you might choose to use a collage of your published stories – or the titles you've worked for could be enough to remind a tardy credit controller that perhaps you should be taken seriously.

Be sure your invoice includes:

THE PUBLICATION'S DETAILS

Publishers will have their own requirements as to what needs to be included on the invoice (company address, tax registration number, invoice number etc). Before you check these requirements with your editor, take a look at your commission form – the details are often included there.

THE GENERAL DETAILS

The date and the client's reference number (or just magazine title and issue number) and your own invoice number. It might simply be superstition, but I never start at 001 for a new client. I'd prefer a junior accounts clerk to jump to the mistaken conclusion from my 'BBC007' invoice number that I'm already an established contributor.

DETAILS OF THE WORK YOU'VE DONE

Include the title of the story, the issue it's scheduled for, the name of the commissioning editor, the agreed word-rate, and the total amount due in the currency in which the publication pays.

YOUR DETAILS

So that payment can be made swiftly, ensure all your basic information is included – your full name, address and contact details. Also, of course, your bank details – account name and number, bank code, bank address, IBAN code and Swift code. Some companies require you include your tax reference number.

TIMEFRAME FOR PAYMENT

This information is not crucial, but it could add weight to your follow-up emails if you have to chase a late payer. Depending on agreements the timeframe for payment might vary between 'payment immediately' to 'payment 90 days after publication'.

§

7

THE WRITER'S STARTING BLOCK

by Mark Eveleigh

If you wait for inspiration to write you're not a writer, you're a waiter.

– Dan Poynter –

After all the work you've put into pitching, researching, travelling, organising, pitching some more, it is – finally – time to sit down and write. Now, this book isn't about *how* to write a travel story, but we do have some valuable advice on how to get your head into the right space for writing memorable travel features you'll be proud of.

THE MYTH OF WRITER'S BLOCK

Being a travel writer might be the best job in the world, but sometimes you still have to work at it. Unless they have a trust fund or private savings, writer's block is a pretentious luxury that few professionals can afford.

At worst, look upon writer's block simply as a sprinter's starting block from which you might occasionally need a push before you can get up and running. There are countless forms that that 'push' might take. No two writers work in identical ways and they will often choose wildly different rhythms and sources of inspiration. According to literary lore Raymond Chandler was inspired to get down to writing by watching his wife doing the housework in the nude. Agatha Christie, meanwhile, believed that the best time to plan a book was while doing the dishes. (Potentially a literary match made in heaven had those two ever gotten together.)

The above are not necessarily sources of inspiration that would work for everyone. As a writer you should be on the lookout for motivational activities or habits that are like the magic lantern that, instead of a genie, discharges the long-awaited muse.

GET MOVING

Not all these habits will necessarily be based around your desk: many writers have put their faith in the sort of passive activity that occupies only part of the mind – such as going for a run, or even just a stroll around the garden. The key is to get your subconscious motivated.

Do this and, as long as you maintain the impetus (in other words, don't get distracted), the creative side of your mind will be sure to follow.

Through 'mindless' physical activity you allow your subconscious an opportunity to dismantle the blocks of the barricade that you've inadvertently built between yourself and the subject you want to cover. Don't overdo it with the exercise though. You need to stop long before exhaustion provides the ideal excuse to postpone the problem of writing until tomorrow.

Unlike brick-laying and open-heart surgery, there's no established *modus operandi* for freelance writing. If you realize that you are most productive between the hours of 2am and 6am then you must capitalize on that. You need to keep your mind open to analyse your strengths, hone your skills and establish your own work patterns if you really intend to carve a sustainable career for yourself as a travel writer.

LOOK FOR INSPIRATION

At times sources of inspiration might come more easily from words than from action. Be open to any possible way to reboot a love of words at times when the 'world's most exciting job' seems to have degenerated into a day-to-day slog.

'Little better than a license to bore, travel-writing is the lowest form of literary self-indulgence,' wrote Paul Theroux. 'Dishonest complaining, creative mendacity, pointless heroics, and chronic posturing, much of it distorted with Munchausen syndrome.'

Let's assume, though, that you're aiming for something substantially more inspiring than travel writing of that sort.

Anything that's written without enthusiasm is likely to be read without enjoyment, so do your best to cultivate the most fragile seedling of inspiration when you sense it starting to grow. And try to remember what provokes those blessed moments when you sense that an idea is growing of its own accord and that the words (the right words) are tumbling onto the page almost faster than you can type. That way, you will end up with a set of reliable habits that kickstart inspiration – these will be the rooting hormone for your ideas the next time you find your writing stuck in a rut.

READ MORE

You might be grasping for motivation to get that first sentence written but you'll soon find that a little help from a trusted friend can go a long way. Reach for one of the greats: Ernest Hemingway is the heavy-hitter if you want inspiration for dialogue; Laurie Lee is the pilgrim-poet if you're striving for descriptive beauty; Hunter S Thompson is unbeatable for sheer, raucous, unpredictable gonzo excitement.

There's nothing to stop you from searching for inspiration online, but beware – the Internet can be the black-hole that swallows your most productive hours.

LEARN TO SEE THINGS DIFFERENTLY

Now and then a commission comes through for a story

you're so desperate to write that you can't wait to get started. Other times, you might struggle to find the first jolt of enthusiasm that will release the flow of words – and when this happens, it can be productive to write something 'just for fun'. (Writers live in a strange world; can you imagine a plumber sabotaging their own water tank on Sunday evening in an effort to work up the enthusiasm to clock in on Monday morning?)

'How vividly you see a strange town or a strange country when you first enter it,' wrote Dorothea Brande in her excellent book *Becoming a Writer*. 'As you get into your streetcar, or walk along a street, tell yourself that for 15 minutes you will notice every single thing that your eyes rest on.' Brande's words were written in 1934 but (apart from the fact that very few of us travel by 'streetcar' these days) her advice still holds true today.

Train yourself to see things with fresh eyes. You don't need to wait for exciting new surroundings to try this exercise. In fact, it's even more beneficial when you force the focus of eyes that are used to looking upon a familiar scene with a jaundiced lack of awareness.

PUT YOUR SUBCONSCIOUS TO WORK

You don't need to book an international ticket to begin your training as a travel writer. Simply head to the nearest busy street, park, market or café. Then find a seat, take out a notebook and simply start to write about your surroundings. Depending on your whim, either describe the scene with journalistic accuracy or feel free to make up fictional personalities or stories based upon passers-by. If you want to practise dialogue, feel free to invent unheard conversations between unsuspecting people around you.

For the purposes of this exercise, what you write is less important than the fact that you keep that pen moving. Simply jotting down impressions can be enough to get the words flowing and as you find yourself getting into a rhythm, begin to concentrate on finding the *mot juste*, the exact phrases that sum up the situations/images/characters you want to portray.

If this exercise is geared at getting psyched to start work on an actual story, then allow that story to sit in the back of your mind but don't allow it to take over the exercise. Instead, push it down and subdue it if it starts to demand attention. The subconscious mind is like a spoiled child that resents being ignored; by actively suppressing this urge to concentrate on the story you're likely to find that it begins to clamour for your attention. But force yourself to decide that you'll listen to it only when you're ready. You can be sure that, by that time, it will be willing to cooperate.

By letting your subconscious get to work without your input you're likely to find that, by the time you've wandered back home, both the professional you and your subconscious will be desperate to get down to work in earnest. The muse has landed.

THE 'PARALLEL WORLDS' WRITING EXERCISE

Freelance writing can be a lonely process but if you're lucky enough to have someone you can share these trials with, then you could find that motivation in these exercises is often enhanced by working in tandem with another writer… if only because you're now committed to concentrating on the project and are less likely to give in to the nagging of your subconscious mind. (Or that suddenly overwhelming urge to tidy out the cupboards, fold the laundry, clean the oven or wash the floors.)

Think of these tandem writing projects as 'parallel world' exercises. One of the most enlightening of these is to sit back-to-back with another writer, so that you're both looking in opposite directions down a busy street. Then, spend exactly 30 minutes writing about the passers-by, sounds, smells, impressions, the view itself.

It's important to set a time limit because it motivates you to write hard and fast. It's not important how many words you get down on paper – only that you should be writing whenever you are not scanning the scene. You'll be likely to notice that, within just a few minutes, the periodic glances you shoot up the street are made with different eyes – eyes that are searching hungrily for imagery that you would not normally have noticed.

An important rule in this exercise is that you are not allowed to poach 'material' that happens behind your back – in what should be considered the other writer's territory. Even if your ears register something dramatic – the clatter of a waiter's falling tray for example, or the unexpected slam of a nearby door – do not turn around. Just record your own impression of what has happened.

This can be incredibly enlightening because when you both compare notes afterwards, you're likely to be astounded by just how different your impressions of the same street were.

It's logical that the views described would be different but, for example, both writers might have described the same people from different angles and recorded entirely different aspects of their characters, or even described their outfit, walk or style in such a way that they might appear unrecognisable. The unique portrayals will have been influenced not only by the viewpoint, but also by each writer's frame of mind. When comparing notes afterwards, it can sometimes be hard to believe that you were both writing about the same location in the same moments.

This exercise is one of the best ways to bully the muse into getting down to work. You might also be astounded to realise just how much you can write within the space of a concentrated 30 minutes. More importantly, however, the parallel world's exercise is a valuable reminder of how your personal reaction to a location could influence your readers.

Been there, says Mark...

You don't need to have a neighbour or family member to share this experience with because these projects can be just as enlightening working remotely with another writer in a completely different town, or even on separate continents.

For example, Narina and I have recorded parallel-world impressions of two different commuter buses on the same morning in cities on opposite sides of the world. We've sat at exactly the same moment in cafés on different continents (Narina in Cape Town, and me 7,000km away in Buenos Aires) and written about the characters around us.

Merely knowing that you've made a commitment to another writer and are now forced to get down to work can be enough to get the muse harnessed back into the yoke.

Established writers who won't type out a word without the promise of a paycheque can benefit just as much as struggling novices from exercises of this sort. Having said that, if you do enough of these exercises the time is likely to come when you realise that there are not enough hours in the day to devote to such purely enjoyable writing bouts. Get into the right habits early on and you may find that by the time your working week is filling up with paid commissions, you've long since tamed the muse. She will be ready to get to work the moment you open a new document for the next story.

THE CAFFEINE-RUSH CHALLENGE

When inspiration wanes sometimes it's simply enough to head for a change of scene. If that change of scene can be matched with a kind of psychological timer then so much the better. (I've tried setting an actual timer, forbidding myself from getting up – or even looking up – for, say, an hour. But that never helped since outside influences such as the telephone or visitors frequently presented interruptions. Or excuses.)

A good ploy can be to head to a café (one where you're unlikely to know anyone) and challenge yourself to write, for example, the first draft of a 1,000-word article in the space of time it takes to drink two cappuccinos. You're likely to realise that you can make more headway during an intense hour in these 'caffeine rush' bouts than you'd manage in an entire day slumped over your desk.

Been there, says Mark...

During the years I was based in Madrid, the bar on the corner became my querencia *when I needed added motivation to get a story underway. I realised that, if I worked hard, I could put together the first draft of a 1,500-word article in the time it took to leisurely drink two pints. (I was still relatively broke at the start of my career, so beer-money was a serious outlay that I could only justify if I convinced myself that I was being highly productive.)*

Hemingway worked on the theory that you should 'write drunk and edit sober' and his good friend F. Scott Fitzgerald apparently complained that any stories he wrote when he was sober were 'stupid'. You can have too much of a good thing though, and I'd normally settle the tab after the second pint and make sure that the second, third and fourth sessions of polishing didn't take place in the bar.

This probably shouldn't be looked upon as a daily solution to your search for motivation. You can't expect to fuel an entire career on booze... unless you're Brendan Behan, that is. Behan, who described himself as a 'drinker with writing problems', once offered to come up with a new marketing slogan for Guinness if they sent him a crate of their finest for every week it took him to work on it. After a delay of several weeks, the marketing representative called around at the Behan residence to find the great writer barely conscious beside the latest delivery: 'Guinness makes you drunk,' Behan slurred.

LEARN TO BE IN TWO PLACES AT ONCE

An obvious part of the skillset of a travel writer is the ability to immerse yourself as completely as possible in a location and a culture. It's less well known that there's a flip side to this; it's the ability to block out everything that's going on around you in the real world so that you can teleport yourself to an entirely different place and time.

You might be on a terrace in Paris, sipping café au lait and tackling a tight deadline that's sending your imagination back to the alleyways of Zanzibar, to catch again the scent of spices from the market and the flicker of the swirling kangas the stallholders wear. Or you might be sitting in a heat-shimmering Kalahari bush camp, writing about Bangkok's bustling Chao Phraya River. Or in a Vietnamese sleeper-train trying to recall the taste of Spanish *jamon serrano*.

The ability to separate two sides of your conscious self is crucial too if you want to harness the editorial half of your mind. This is that half that Dorothea Brande described as 'your common sense, everyday character'. (This is the sensible half that probably discouraged your decision to undertake this career in the first place).

'The writer (like every artist),' Brande wrote, 'is a dual

personality. In him the unconscious flows freely…Each side of his character must learn to be able to trust the other to do what is in its field and to carry the full responsibility for its own work.'

You need to collaborate with this surly stick-in-the-mud part of your character so that it will give you its honest reactions to your writing. This side of your character is almost certainly the harshest critic you'll ever come in contact with. At least, let's hope so.

Paul Theroux recalls that his mother wrote him a long letter when his first book was published: 'She said the book was a piece of trash,' he recalled. 'That was her exact word. Trash! Thanks Mom!'

Been there, says Narina…

When I'm on assignment I often snap what, at the time, seems to be very random photographs – a quick pic of a busy street, or a row of market stalls, or the flowerbeds in a park. The photos aren't composed, and they're usually simply snapped while I'm on the move.

Although I'd never use these images for publication, I load them to the same Lightroom folder as the polished images from that assignment and when I sit down to write (which could be months later), I revisit that folder often.

Scrolling through the images is a great way to take my mind back to that place – and the 'random' photos become particularly useful in reminding me of the everyday details that will bring colour and a sense of place into my feature.

WRITE ACCORDING TO A SCHEDULE

For a 1,000-word travel feature most editors will give you at least a clear week to get the story finished. It can often be longer but there are times when you might have to file copy the same day. (In an ideal world such tight deadlines would be unnecessary, but they should be looked upon as a gift for every jobbing freelancer; for every ridiculously tight deadline you get it's likely that one of your competitors proved unreliable.)

Usually, you can negotiate a slightly higher payrate for such a tight deadline (often double the usual fee). What is even more important in the long run though is that, by saving the situation, you stand a great chance of being the go-to writer for future features.

Been there, says Mark...

Personally, I'd always prefer a tight deadline to no deadline. When I know I have to file an article by a given day I'll refuse to be late. Ever. If, however, an editor tells me that there's no hurry and I should file 'whenever convenient'...well, then that article might be hanging over my head unwritten for weeks.

Assuming you've already made the trip so you have the material and have read up and researched fully, a reasonable one-week timeline for producing an average length piece (let's say 1,500 words) might look something like this:

- Day 1 – Write the first draft.
- Day 2 – Write the second draft.
- Day 3 – Write another draft if necessary, or polish what you already have. Send fact-checking emails out to the experts and sources to make sure they're happy with quotes you've included, and to clarify any factual doubts you might have.
- Day 4 – Polish and fine-tune while you wait for fact-checking and the thumbs-up on quotes. (People are often slow to reply so you can't leave the emails too late.)
- Day 5 – Don't even look at the story. Work on something totally unrelated instead. Rest assured though that your subconscious mind will still be hard at work reviewing this piece even on this 'day off'. (In reality, you will often have two or three articles in production simultaneously and a change of tack will help to refresh your thought processes.)
- Day 6 – You'll be surprised how often your subconscious mind will have picked up errors or holes in the story line. You can address these now and also add any changes that have come from your experts and sources. Give the copy a final polish and listen to the whole thing using a text-to-voice or 'read aloud' tool. Finally, get a trusted critic to read it through. Fresh eyes and an honest opinion make all the difference.
- Day 7 – Consider changes suggested by your trusted critic. Listen to the entire article again using that wonderful text-to-voice tool – it's amazing how much this helps. Once you're happy, file the copy.

As you can see from this schedule, a deadline of a week might really only entail five solid days working on the feature. Articles of around 3,000 words will take longer, of course, but if you stick to roughly the same programme you should find that they are still achievable in less than two weeks.

Been there, says Narina…

Mark's given some valuable advice on how to structure your time when writing a feature – but to be honest, this doesn't work for me. At all.

You see, I write in a very different way. I usually have to get my first paragraph absolutely perfect before I can flow with the rest of the feature. It's not a great way to work because I could spend two days agonising over the pacing, the intrigue, the emotion of those first few sentences – but once that clicks into place, the rest of the writing process is usually pretty smooth-going for me.

When I'm really stuck with the narrative then I'll often get words on the page by starting with any fact boxes or sidebars that the editor has asked for. This helps my brain click into gear, and once those essentials have been written I know what word count I'm aiming at for the narrative.

I edit the feature as I go along and so while Mark has various drafts of a feature, I only ever work on my one, polished version of the story. Any sentences or paragraphs that don't work are deleted from that polished version after they've been copy-pasted into an 'extras' document, so that I can retrieve them later on if necessary.

THE BASICS OF A TRAVEL FEATURE

When you file your copy, make sure it is as neat and error-free as possible. The following points should help you create a document that not only looks professional, but that reads well, too:

LABEL YOUR WORK

At the top of the document include a title, your name and the name of the commissioning editor.

INCLUDE AN INTRO

An intro, blurb or 'lede' in old newspapermen's jargon, sits right at the beginning of the feature (just under the title); it gives the reader a taster of the subject and identifies the reporter. Not all freelancers supply this with their copy but the editor is likely to appreciate a contributor who takes the time to supply a lede (along with a suggested title).

DON'T START WITH 'I'

Never, under any circumstance, begin the main story (the 'body copy') with the word 'I'. No matter where you go from there, you've opened by implying that this feature will be more about you than about the destination or subject you're writing about.

DON'T START AT THE BEGINNING

The mark of an inexperienced travel writer is the desire to tell the story from the moment they got off the plane. Or, worse, when they woke up that morning.

HOOK THE READER WITH THE FIRST SENTENCE

You can do this by starting with a dramatic or thrilling incident, or by leading in with an intriguing quote that makes the reader want to read on to see what develops.

STATE THE LOCATION

Regardless of what is explained in the lede, it's wise to drop a general clue into the first paragraph so that your readers are aware from the outset what geographical region and situation you're teleporting them into. Then, somewhere around the third paragraph you need to explain the location and situation in greater detail.

SURPRISE THE READER

Never assume that the reader is familiar with the topic you're writing about – but at the same time, imagine that one or two of the readers will be world-renowned experts on the subject. Now try to include a few real nuggets of information (astounding, but uncontestably true) that are likely to come as a surprise even to those readers. If a reader (*any* reader) comes to the end of your feature having learned *nothing* whatsoever, then you've failed.

INCLUDE ATMOSPHERIC DIALOGUE

Break the monotony of big blocks of text with lively quotes and interactions with people who are central to the story. There are no fixed rules to writing and, in any case, it's often said that the greatest writers are those who know how and when to break the rules.

Many inexperienced writers are uncomfortable about attempting to reproduce conversations, but it's a skill that the travel writer should practise and, as much as possible, perfect. Quote accurately but write in such a way that the dialogue seems natural and at the same time provides an insight into the speaker's character.

Eaves-drop on any cocktail party and you'll notice that most people waffle and warble to their heart's content before they get to the point. When a writer is expected to reproduce such dialogue within the confines of a tightly woven 1,000-word article, it's almost always necessary to paraphrase to some extent. If this is the case, you should always take time to check before you file the copy to be sure that your sources are happy with how they've been quoted.

Keep in mind that while it is absolutely *not acceptable* to change the meaning of what someone is saying, it is usually considered okay to edit someone's sentences respectfully if English is not their mother-tongue.

CHECK THE FACTS

Fact-check every detail with reliable sources. These days the old warning about not believing everything you read is truer than ever. There are thousands of sloppily written, hurriedly researched and badly edited blogs (and articles) out there produced by people who portray themselves as experts… always bear in mind that a fact does not become an unarguable truth just because it has been repeated 500,000 times on the Internet. (For more on this see chapter 8.)

If you've quoted anyone, send them the copy to check that you didn't mishear or misunderstand, and that they haven't been taken out of context.

CONSIDER THE CONSEQUENCES

Keep in mind the possible implications of your writing. Your breathless first-person adventure snippet on being robbed in Barcelona / Rio / NYC / Nairobi could dissuade travellers from going there, potentially affecting the livelihood of thousands of people. Do your best to support ethical hotels and operators who have the welfare of local communities and environments at heart. (Wherever possible either congratulate them on this effort or encourage them to take their laudable claims to greater levels).

EXPERIMENT WITH THE FLOW OF THE STORY

Sometimes you might want to write the ending of your article before the middle section. Often your evocative starting point might provide you with a wonderful ending. This can work very well but if the story is much over 1,000 words you might want to insert a reminder or two part-way through the copy, just to be sure that the reader hasn't forgotten that initial teaser of suspense. Then you can 'circle back' to tie in with your opening drama / dialogue at the end of the article.

INCLUDE COPY FOR TEXT BOXES

The requirements for 'box out' sections and fact boxes differ for every publication, but usually include smaller side-articles covering aspects of the main story, or details such as where to eat or sleep, or important sights to visit. If these are required, the editor will usually give full details at the commissioning stage.

Narina finds it useful to work on these boxes before she starts to write the body of her feature. She says it's a great way to get her head back into a place – plus, once these are complete, she knows exactly what word count the main section of the feature should be.

LIST YOUR SOURCES

When you file your copy, it is worth including links to the sources of reliable information that confirm your facts. This will reassure the editor and save the sub-editors (whose job it usually is to fact check) from having to contact you to confirm every unexpected point you've included.

GIVE YOUR HEAD SOME SPACE

Allowing ample time for the piece to stew and simmer is vital if you're to avoid becoming punch-drunk with it. When you're punch-drunk with a story you start to read what you *think* is on the screen and not what is *actually* there. Using that 'read aloud' or 'text-to-speech' tool is an excellent way to sidestep those pitfalls.

Search out an unbiased critic who is prepared to read the copy and give you honest feedback. Every writer craves literary praise, but the 'honest critic' you ask to read through your feature should, ideally, be another writer rather than your mum who, doubtless, loves everything you do anyway.

You can't write 10 hours day after day on a single story without getting punch-drunk so you need to work on other things that are just as much a part of your business. When you're not actually working on a story, you'll be answering emails, working on pitches or travel itineraries, or researching. You should make time each day for reading too, since you can't expect to be a writer without also being a reader. Regardless, you should try to ensure that you write *something* every single day.

Few freelance travel writers regularly observe weekends. Most just snag a few rest days here and there, whenever the obligations of assignments or writing allow. Travel days (almost invariably unpaid) are often taken as days off… unless you have a tight deadline that has to be beaten in airport lounges or mid-air.

Perhaps we should have mentioned earlier too that sick leave, paid holidays and pension programs are not normally a part of the job description of a freelance writer. If that's a deal-breaker, you should probably stop reading at this point.

Been there, says Narina...

This is a good place to jump in and have a quick word about cliches – because travel features can be full of them. 'The cosy chalet was nestled into the base of rolling green hills'... it's enough to make any self-respecting editor (or reader, or writer) groan and throw down a magazine in disgust.

The thing is, it's so easy to use a cliché (particularly when your brain is tired). Those little words and phrases are often so embedded in our brains that the automatic response to using one word is often to add the rest of the cliché. Water? Crystal clear. Town? Sleepy. City? Bustling. Chalet? Cosy. We often do it without thinking.

And that's the problem: we do it without thinking. Clichés are an indication of lazy writing.

My advice on how to avoid using clichés is always this: write your story and then set it aside for a day. You need this break so that you're not reading your writing on autopilot. When you come back to it, highlight the phrases that stand out as obvious clichés, or as being words that you wouldn't use in conversation with a friend. You'll either have worked too hard to put that phrase together, or else you've not had to think about it at all, and you've fallen into a cliché.

Once you've done this, find a more specific way of saying what's been highlighted). Using a thesaurus might help to trigger some inspiration.

BEAT YOUR DEADLINE

Always meet your deadline. Sure, there might be, once in a blue moon, dire extenuating circumstances that make you file your copy late – but bear in mind that for every deadline you fail to meet, there will be a more reliable competitor ready to step into your shoes.

That said, if something's not gone according to plan (unavoidable travel delays for example) and you know you won't be able to meet your deadline, then contact your editor immediately and ask if they have leeway to give you a few extra days on the deadline. Knowing far in advance that the copy will be filed later than initially expected will allow the editorial team to adjust their workflow accordingly.

Been there, says Mark...

One of my best-paying assignments during my first couple of years as a freelancer was a miraculously lucrative US$4,000 writing gig for a story for the now-defunct Escapes Magazine *on my Madagascar expedition. I needed the money so badly that I checked myself out of Madrid hospital's malaria ward so that I could stagger home to my solitary apartment to get the copy filed on time.*

Narina says that from an editor's point of view asking for an extension on the deadline would have been acceptable, but it felt like a watershed in my career to be writing for this title and I didn't want to rock any boats.

EXPECT CHANGES FROM THE EDITOR

A great writer deserves a proficient editor. An inexperienced writer *needs* one. That said, it's your job to get the article 100% perfect, and it should be your ambition to have every feature accepted without any changes at all. There are no excuses for spelling mistakes and grammatical errors – nor is there any excuse for factual mistakes (see chapter 8).

Writing, like any other artform, is largely a matter of taste and perception, however, so there could well be some changes suggested or requested by the editor. This is normal… but if an editor ever asks for a major rewrite, know that you've failed to live up to expectations.

§

8

TIPS AND TOOLS
FOR RESEARCH

by Mark Eveleigh

*Being a good writer is 3% talent,
97% not being distracted by the
Internet.*

– Anonymous –

Limits of reliable information. This is what was printed on
the most detailed maps I could find when I lead my first
expedition into Central Borneo in 1995. These days the
entire area we crossed in that two-month jungle trip can

be visited virtually within seconds on Google Earth, instantly revealing valleys and peaks that, even to this day, have never been visited by other outsiders.

With Google Earth what you see is pretty much what you get, but this is not always the case with Internet research in general. As the Internet becomes increasingly packed with information it seems, paradoxically, that *mis*-information becomes exponentially commoner than ever. This is because the lazy practise of cut-and-paste journalism is the only answer to tighter, increasingly competitive, deadlines. Winning the race to be the first to report has become more important than the obligation to report correctly.

If you're going to be doing online research (which, let's face it, you almost certainly will), then it's a good idea to save bookmarks to sites that can be considered, if not infallible, then at least reliable. Or, failing that, maybe just 'reputable'.

Your 'reliable sources' folder might contain links to such sites as History Encyclopaedia, CIA World Factbook, National Geographic, Britannica, British Museum website, Guinness Book of Records, UNESCO and WWF. (I've found wildly conflicting facts and figures from these last two but it's safe to say that if you quote data from these sources few editors will doubt your accuracy.) Wikipedia is not likely to be accepted as a reliable source by most editors but, since that site also lists its references, it can be used as a valuable staging-post for tracking down original sources.

Nothing should ever be taken entirely for granted

and your best sources are likely to be experts in the field – who you can then quote directly: a naturalist or guide would be perfect for a wildlife-focussed travel story; a local chef for a foodie angle; an anthropologist or, perhaps better still, a tribal elder for a cultural story… Whoever you choose, treat their comments with respect.

Most reputable publications will have a sub-editor whose job it is to fact-check every detail of a story. You can save them and (more importantly *yourself*) a lot of time by keeping notes of sources as you write, and adding a list of links to the end of the feature so that the sub-editor can verify without having to contact you with a whole string of queries.

It's worthwhile recording these sources as you work because after you've spent three days scouring through books, articles and online info it can be a frustrating mission to have to track down the original source of a snippet of info you've included as a key fact in your story.

Been there, says Mark…

I'd been commissioned to write a feature on Maasai beadwork from Kenya. There was one particularly colourful snippet of information that had been woven into the thread of almost every single piece of writing I found online about the Maasai's iconic craft. This piece of information was apparently purely fictitious but (presumably solely because it was as vibrantly colourful as the beads themselves) it had been copied and pasted into pretty much every information source on the subject.

My own commissioning editor was also enamoured with that snippet of information, but the local experts I spoke to (including several tribal elders) specifically asked me not to perpetuate this nonsense which, they believed, had simply been invented decades ago by some imaginative guide.

It seems that if something is repeated enough times on the Internet it actually becomes the accepted truth. It's almost impossible to break such a chain of misinformation once it gets started but, fortunately, I managed to convince the editor that we should stick to incontrovertible facts that had come straight from the horse's mouth.

When you're setting out to write a travel feature, what you write is more important than how you write it. Think about it: if the most basic purpose of a publication is to convey information, and if the facts in your story are incorrect or unclear, you've not done your job.

Of course, being able to get that info across in an interesting, entertaining way is essential – but before you put your fingers on the keyboard and begin to wax lyrical, there are a few things you should know:

DO YOUR RESEARCH – THOROUGHLY

It's very easy to tell when someone has written about unfamiliar territory: the copy is vague and confusing. If you don't understand what you're writing about, your story will read as a jumble of paraphrases, clichés and out-of-context quotes. Do your research thoroughly and understand what you're writing about before you type the first word – you'll find the process of writing becomes easier.

GO TO THE MOST DIRECT SOURCE

It's easy to turn to the Internet when you need information – but be careful. When you start to venture deep into Google, you'll see how many websites contain exactly the same paragraphs of information – people have blindly copied and pasted and the info you end up relying on may be out of date or incorrect.

GO TO THE MOST DIRECT AND RELIABLE SOURCE

For the most basic information for travel writing, official tourism boards and well-established guidebooks may be your best starting point.

PICK UP THE PHONE

Email has long been the default setting when it comes to communication. If you're interviewing someone for a story or requesting information then it's good to have this written record – however, making a personal connection by speaking to someone before you email them can be invaluable.

Here are four reasons to pick up the phone:

• People are likely to put more effort into an email response when they're writing to someone they 'know'.

• If they can't answer your question, they could direct you to someone who can – no time wasted.

• Tell them on the phone that you'll email questions through to them, and they'll know to look out for it – your email will be less likely to get lost in their inbox.

• If you need to clarify something simple, it's usually easier and faster to discuss it on the phone.

LEARN TO LET GO

It's so easy to get caught up in research – and often, an inexperienced writer will battle to draw what they need from the reams of information they gather.

They might start out reading about trails in Cape Town for a story on day walks; next thing they're getting to grips with the geological composition of Table Mountain, and before long their feature becomes an encyclopaedia of the landscapes of the Western Cape.

Learn to sift carefully through the information you gather, pick out what is most interesting and relevant to the feature and don't be scared to let go of the details that don't enhance your story.

§

9

HOW THE FINANCES WORK

by Mark Eveleigh

We're really all of us bottomly broke...I haven't had time to work in weeks.

– Jack Kerouac –

In a perfect world you should never write unless you're inspired. For a professional, however, this can't *always* be true. Only romantic amateurs (or poets with trust funds) imagine that it is a corruption of the 'art of writing' for a professional to write because they have bills to pay. But this book is dedicated to professionals.

Sometimes you simply have to write because it's what you do *for a living*.

Occasionally you'll be commissioned to write features that you care very little about – but look on those gigs as the bread and butter that will allow you the freedom later to write stories that you think really deserve to be told. You can't expect that your words are going to save the world, but all serious writers appreciate the thought that something they write – maybe a conservation piece or a cultural story about a struggling community – might someday lead to a change for the better.

Been there, says Mark...

Many of the stories I've been proudest of were written for the long-gone CNN Traveller *magazine back in the days when it was the inflight magazine of Air Force One. I wrote 20 or more features for that magazine on such aspects as corruption in India's tiger reserves, the plight of Southeast Asia's dispossessed Bajau Laut (aka 'Sea Gypsies'), the dangers facing African immigrants on mafia-run Moroccan 'Death Boats' and jaguar conservation in Costa Rica. It was an added incentive in writing those pieces to know that Barak Obama and his team might think that a few of these were problems worth dealing with.*

Then again, for every 'worthwhile' commission of that sort there are likely to be five or six others that I'd write simply to pay the bills. It's relatively hard (for me at least) to find inspiration in a commission to write about '24 Hours in Kuala Lumpur / Panama City / Delhi…' or even 'Bali's best secret beaches' or 'A round-up of Rajasthan's most colourful towns'. Such stories are normally (but not always) relatively small payers so they tend to be written from existing travel experiences, backed up with online research. Apart from the fact that such an article might make life a little easier for tourism workers or communities in those areas, it's hard to feel that your writing talents are being used for the 'greater good'.

WHAT CAN YOU EXPECT TO EARN?

For the lucky (and super-talented) few there might be millions to be made, but this business is best described as the world's most wonderful way to enjoy being poor. It is, however, an excellent choice for someone who rates the importance of quality of life over that of salary.

For a national UK national newspaper the payrate is usually around £350 (US$480) per 1,000 words, and a long feature might stretch across 3,000 words. The lower and higher ends of the scale for 1,000-word magazine feature range from under US$300 to US$1,500. Occasionally (especially if it's a bulk order from a regular client who's paying for several stories) you might accept US$300 for a 1,000-word feature but this might, on a fortunate day, sometimes be balanced by a commission that could net US$3,000 or more.

Bear in mind that these figures are boosted (sometimes doubled) if you combine your writing with photography (more on this in chapter 11).

LESS CAN SOMETIMES BE MORE

Back in 1997 I was producing around 60 full-length articles a year because I had several regular titles I worked for (some almost on a weekly basis). They were valued clients but their rates were not great and since I was producing articles at such speed, I had little time to pitch to bigger payers. Just as importantly, I began to worry that the quality of my work might be slipping.

One day I made a business decision to stop pitching the smaller payers. I drew the line at US$700 an article and began only to chase publications that paid rates higher than that. A year later I was making substantially more income – even though I only produced about 40 articles. A few years later I made a similar decision and again trimmed off the lower payers (refusing commissions that paid less than US$1,000). The following year was financially better still, and I was far happier with the work I was producing.

Regular work is a godsend for a freelance writer and it is nerve-racking to turn your back on any prospective work. It was a revelation to realise that, when I summoned the courage to aim higher, less could actually be more.

WHO WILL COVER
YOUR TRAVEL EXPENSES?

Your travel costs can be minimised – or sometimes erased entirely – if you work with a flight company, a tour operator or a PR agency (see chapter 10).

These days very few magazines cover expenses, and the few that do will almost always cap a maximum limit. Very few publications have a blank cheque for covering freelance expenses on travel assignments and most claim that they balance their rates to cover the costs of the assignment. However, the rates that publications pay very rarely cover the costs involved in setting up a long international trip so, to make a trip really profitable, you're going to need to sell several features from each trip.

If you've worked for an editor or publication on a fairly regular basis, you might take a chance and point out politely that an upcoming assignment is likely to be unusually expensive. In such cases many editors are able to find a little extra budget.

In the rare event that expenses *are* covered, you'd probably be expected to file your receipts along with your expenses claim. I find that prepaid 'tap-and-pay' cards are a convenient way of minimising the number of receipts needed – in Singapore, for example, MRT travel cards can also be charged and used in outlets like the ubiquitous Seven-Eleven grocery stores as well as on public transport. The Uber app – or, in Asia, Grab – is another great way to keep all your taxi costs conveniently filed in the same online account.

Been there, says Mark...

When I was working on a series of features around Southeast Asia, I took to carrying around my own receipt book. It turned out to be crucial since I was travelling in remote areas and very few tuk-tuk drivers, trishaw riders or street food cooks could have been expected to write a receipt in English. Needless to say I was never tempted to 'cook' that little black book, but it was far easier to fill in the details myself and simply ask for a signature.

The magazine's accountant was presumably grateful for such a tidy system since he never questioned the fact that all details seemed to be written in the same scrawling script known locally as cakar ayam *(chicken scratches).*

HOW IS THE PAYRATE FOR PHOTOS CALCULATED?

Most magazines quote a per-word rate and then have a standard rate for images, which is usually based on the size that an image is used (an eighth of a page, quarter page, half page, full page, DPS or double-page spread, and cover). As a ballpark average figure these days, this could be around US$70 for a quarter-page image, stretching up to around US$400 for a double-page-spread in a travel magazine.

Sometimes you can convince an editor to agree a price for a words-and-pics package. Your price might have to be more competitive, but in this way you're guaranteeing that your images will be used with your story (which is much better for your portfolio).

COMPROMISE ON RATES
FOR YOUR REGULAR CLIENTS

It can be tempting to accept lower-paying commissions when you know that the invoice is going to be settled very promptly or if there is an opportunity for ongoing regular work.

Many years ago, I was approached by a respected safari company who asked if I'd agree to be listed as a 'safari expert' and to write reviews of any African national parks or reserves I visited. The payrate was only about US$300/1,000 words but, since these clients *always* pay their invoices within 24 hours, it meant an almost instant source of much-appreciated income as soon as I returned from an assignment. I've since done more than 40 reviews for them from different parks and reserves.

WHEN WILL YOU GET PAID?

Publishing companies tend to have their own payment systems and it is they – not you, the freelancer –who will dictate the terms. It's quite rare these days for magazines to pay for copy on submission; it's more common to be paid 30 days after publication, while some pay 60 days after publication. This means that because of the timeline of a magazine cycle (see chapter 4 for more on this), you can often expect to be paid for your copy three or four months after you've submitted it.

THE MIXED BLESSINGS
OF THE SLOW PAYER

When you come across a prompt payer, hang onto them like you would the goose that lays the golden egg. It might surprise you, however, to realise that there's a benefit for the established freelancer in clients who pay long after publication.

If a company pays 60 days after publication, you might only get paid five or six months after you forked out on the expenses to cover your trip. It's not in the nature of most travel addicts to save 'for a rainy day.' (We're more likely just to blow the money on a ticket to the sun.) Few would-be travel writers can afford therefore to sit out four months on the breadline while they wait for the first payment to come in.

Slow payers are probably the number one factor in driving would-be freelancers to search for 'proper jobs' with regular pay packets. There's a 'competition-limiting' advantage for a seasoned freelancer in this delay: once you're on a roll it makes little difference if you're getting paid for the majority of your features two, four or six months after you covered the costs of the trip. Maybe you're already in Kenya when the Thailand payments come through, and are in Colombia when the Kenya stories are paid up.

The initial period can be tough, as it is with most self-employed people. If you can just survive the first year on the breadline, the delay starts to make little difference. Sometimes an escape route is the worst thing for scuppering plans, and only those who are completely committed to waiting it out (or have no alternatives) tend to get through this period. After all, if you're going to jump it's usually safest to jump into deep water.

CAN A SINGLE COMMISSION MAKE A TRIP PROFITABLE?

The best payers certainly make it worthwhile travelling anywhere in the world on assignment. As a general rule though, I pitch for an angle on a trip before departure and as long as I get at least one decent commission then I can be 90% certain that the trip will be financially viable. If that first commission covers (or *mostly* covers) the costs of the trip then I can hope that subsequent features will represent my actual profit.

Sometimes it's less of a business than a game of roulette. I once set off on a 10-day horse-back safari around Botswana's Tuli Circle with just one confirmed commission (from *CNN Traveller* magazine). I figured it was enough to break even on the trip even if I couldn't get any other commissions. Over the next couple of years I wrote 14 full-length features about that 10-day trip, making it my most successful assignment ever.

You can never be entirely sure about long-term appeal, though, and it's often frustratingly hard to anticipate which trips might fall flat. A few years ago Narina and I set up an assignment in a remote part of Myanmar's Shan State. We were apparently only the second foreigners to pass through the area since the army had closed opium operations in that region. We figured it would have been a story we could publish widely – but we managed to sell just two features on that trip. Even though the journey was hosted we barely broke even after we paid for our flights and sundry expenses, such as tips for guides.

REPUBLISH YOUR WORK

Once a story has been published, you're entirely free to do as many re-writes as you want to. With very clever marketing you might find that it is possible to place previously published stories with lower-paying titles that are unable to afford custom-written pieces. There are not many titles who will take previously published features, however, and with so many magazines running print stories on blogs and websites these days, the options are even more limited.

BE AWARE OF ONLINE
AND SYNDICATION RIGHTS

Back in the 1990s websites began to worm their way inconspicuously into magazine and newspaper businesses – almost without anyone apart from web-gurus even noticing. Suddenly we looked up and there they were, a part of our everyday life.

Today many magazines make more revenue from their websites than they do from print. Others have abandoned print entirely in favour of more lucrative online presence. Only very rarely, however, will a contributor be paid as much for an online story as they would have been offered for the same amount of copy for use in a print issue. I've written sometimes for BBC and CNN websites (which have clicks numbering well into the millions) but the rate is usually about a quarter of what I'd normally expect for the same work for various BBC- and CNN-branded magazines I've contributed to.

The paradox is clear: if you're commissioned to write for a magazine's website you can expect to be paid, but if you've been hired to write for print it's often tacitly expected that the same story can be used online for free. Yet stories that would have effectively disappeared from the public domain after a month in print are sometimes still online a decade later.

There seems to be little that a freelancer can do about this, but you should check whether the story you've been commissioned to write for print will also run on the magazine's website, because this will limit your potential to re-sell it (either in original version or, if the story reaches enough readers over time, perhaps even as a complete rewrite). Although things might change in the future, most freelancers accept this situation and prefer to keep a valuable client happy rather than rock the boat by refusing to allow online reproduction.

Along with online rights, be sure to check what a contract stipulates regarding world rights and syndication.

Been there, says Mark...

Many years ago I covered a West Africa travel story for a leading UK newspaper (who should remain nameless since they've recently adopted a much fairer agreement with contributors). I'd worked for this publication before, but they'd recently updated their contract and demanded rights to republish the story throughout their syndication network. Perhaps naively, I simply signed on the dotted line.

The contract offered no inkling of just how far-reaching their syndication network was... and, anyway, I'd probably have lost the assignment had I refused to sign.

The end result was that the 1,500-word story I wrote for them – for a fairly mediocre payrate – later ran in major newspapers all over the world. I received no extra payment for any of this and, worse still, the story was now so widely spread that I was unable to write about it subsequently for any other publication.

To make matters even worse, as I write this (15 years after the print story ran) my original text, which is now ridiculously out-dated, still sits on the UK newspaper's website.

STRETCH YOUR INCOME
BY LIVING ON LOCATION

In this career the freedom to live and work almost anywhere in the world means that you can also capitalise on spending more time in cheaper locations, where your income will stretch much further.

A freelance travel writer based in London, Paris or

Boston is likely to earn exactly the same as one based in Cusco, Zanzibar or Chiang Mai. The best way to stretch your income is to choose to live in a location that's not only more affordable, but which is also likely to reap a rich harvest in terms of inspiring stories. If that location is also within easy access of a good travel-hub then you're in an even stronger position.

Been there, says Mark...

When I first became a freelance travel journalist back in 1996, I instantly became so poor that I could no longer afford to take flights in search of stories.

Fortunately, I'd moved to Madrid so I wrote articles from around Spain (mostly hitchhiking and sleeping rough). For a fistful of pesetas I could hop on a night-bus to Algeciras ferry-terminal and I'd be in Tangier for breakfast. In Morocco I could at least afford a room. These were the days before low-cost airlines made international flights affordable for most. Today it would be much cheaper to fly to Morocco than to travel overland and even long-haul tickets can be had at prices that are often ludicrously low.

During that period I wrote only about Spain and Morocco (polishing both my Spanish and French at the same time) because I simply couldn't afford to go farther. Within two years I was being paid enough to start making long-haul trips again and two years after that, I was already spending upwards of six months of each year on assignments in various far-flung parts of the world.

§

10

PRESS TRIPS AND SPONSORS

by Mark Eveleigh

*Those of us that had been up all
night were in no mood for coffee
and donuts, we wanted strong drink.
We were, after all, the cream of the
national sporting press.*

– Hunter S Thompson –

Sponsored or complimentary trips can be a thorny issue
and one that I'd almost rather avoid altogether. It's an
important one to address however, because the bottom
line is that with publication payrates often being so dire,

it would be impossible for most travel writers to afford to do what is central to their jobs: travel. Of course, writing about a trip that you've gone on 'for free' brings up some ethical issues, and we'll touch on those in this chapter too.

Some publications claim that they *never* accept stories from comped (free) trips. Bizarrely, it often seems to be high-end, luxury titles that are strictest about the rule forbidding comped trips. If you want to retain diplomatic relations with editors, it is invariably best to refrain from enquiring how trips that apparently cost tens of thousands of dollars regularly appear in magazines that only pay $1,000 for freelance articles.

The average reader might never register this bizarre paradox, but the end result is that somewhere along the line editors are going to have to bend that rule because few professional travel writers can afford to take multi-thousand-dollar 'holidays'.

Many assignments I've undertaken wouldn't have been remotely feasible if I had to pay for the trip myself. I've had several assignments covering week-long voyages on superyachts that cost upwards of US$12,000 for a single night. It doesn't take an accountant to realise that, even at US$4,000 a story (a *highly* optimistic rate), an assignment like that is *never* going to turn a profit. In fact, those stories simply could *never* have been told unless they were comped.

An editor at a leading US newspaper* told me recently that they go a step further and stipulate that they won't hire any travel writer who has undertaken a comped trip within the past three years. Show me a freelancer who hasn't been hosted in three years and I'll show you a freelancer who's been out of work.

*That same newspaper once published a West Africa story of mine that had been syndicated through a major newspaper in the UK. I wrote that story from a comped trip that had been set up with the permission of the UK editor. So, maybe there are more ways to bend that golden rule than are immediately apparent.

Been there, says Narina...

The majority of editors I've worked with on a regular basis are very aware that the rates they're able to pay don't go very far when it comes to covering travel expenses (not to mention other costs like rent, travel insurance, taxes and equipment). They're usually happy for me to include in my feature a mention of places I've stayed at free of charge (or, as I prefer to think of it, people and places I've worked with in order to cover the story) as long as the accommodation or service offered is relevant and recommendable.

What's important is how the mention is written into the feature, as an editorial piece should never read like an advertorial (a paid-for piece of editorial). There are various ways to do this: a story on food in Madrid, for example, could include an interview with a hotel's chef; the details of a travel company could be included in the feature's fact file; as a box at the end of a feature, a hotel's head concierge could give recommendations that tie in with the story. Some publications do run reviews of sorts – and these, it goes without saying, should also always be honest and impartial.

THE ETHICS OF COMPED TRIPS

It is entirely unethical for a travel writer to promise positive exposure in return for a free flight, trip, accommodation or any other sort of remuneration. It is commonly said that, at the current rate, a short mention in a national newspaper is worth around US$1,400 but any hotel, airline, tour operator or tourism board that hosts a journalist (either a press trip or a solo trip) must accept that the journalist remains a totally unbiased reporter and is free to tell the truth entirely.

Any trip or property that turns out to be unrecommendable is likely to see one of two outcomes: the story will be written up truthfully, warts and all, or the story will simply be pulled and will never see the light of day.

In a perfect world the first outcome would be the most just. In effect though, the second outcome is much more common. This is logical because very few travel publications want to waste valuable pages on describing a trip that their readers *won't* want to take.

Been there, says Mark...

I recently undertook an assignment to write about an organisation running anti-poaching patrols in South Africa. The article had been commissioned in advance and all that remained was for me to join a unit on a dawn-patrol in Big Five country for first-hand experience into how the charity operated. New York Times *and* National Geographic *(among many others) had sung the praises of this organisation, so it was almost a foregone conclusion that it would be highly laudable. It was an initiative with so many community benefits that, although I forced myself to keep an open mind, I was almost predisposed to add my recommendation.*

I was so unimpressed that I told my editors it would be immoral for the publication to appear to endorse the organisation by running the article. Unfortunately for everyone concerned, the story had to be pulled. It was bad news for me because I'd sunk three days into the trip and now I was turning my back on valuable income. (Afterwards the editor was fair-minded enough to realise that I'd acted ethically and agreed to pay the expenses and a 50% kill fee).

The other problem was that I had to explain the reasons for the story being pulled to the founder of the organisation. He was understandably disappointed but later complimented me on my ethics and promised that if I took the time to return, I'd see an improvement. There was little point in this, however, since I would have no way of knowing if things had genuinely improved, or if the organisation had simply raised a denser smokescreen between visiting journalists and staff on the ground.

PRESS TRIPS

Many freelancers travel on several group press trips each year. Others avoid them at all costs. ('Is *nothing* cut-and-dried in this business?' I hear you cry.)

THE BENEFITS OF GOING ON A PRESS TRIP

• PR organisations favour bulk press trips because

they're perceived to minimise hassle and expense while maximising exposure.

• They can be a great way for a travel journalist to network and to get to know other journos (and more importantly, editors).

• Press trips can be so comprehensive that you get to see absolutely everything a destination has to offer.

• From a purely experiential point of view, high-end press trips are sometimes a rare chance to travel at a spectacular VIP level. (For several years I travelled on a series of Land Rover press trips – to Spain, Mongolia, Argentina and Oman. We enjoyed business-class flights and private jet transfers, and the trips themselves were a combination of challenging 4x4 desert- and mountain-driving and luxury living. Nevertheless, Land Rover had enough faith in their products never to pressure for 'good coverage'.)

THE PITFALLS OF PRESS TRIPS

• A well-coordinated press trip might see a dozen or more competing writers on location. They will all return home with more or less the same angles to pitch, frequently to the same editors. This leads to a potential drop in income for them all. (Having said that, I once joined a week-long press trip on Indian trains – a combined cadre of Russian and British journalists – and subsequently published 11 features from that trip).

• For any discerning traveller with a wish to become immersed in a location, the disadvantages of a group tour are obvious. You may reason that it is different when the group is made up of supposedly 'worldly' and experienced travel writers, but this often makes surprisingly little difference.

• Press trips can be so exhaustive that you get to see absolutely everything a destination has to offer. (Yes, this was listed as a benefit in the section above). Often so much is crammed into a press trip itinerary that you don't have the time to soak up the atmosphere, to do *real* research or to focus on that single startling aspect of the trip that offers potential for the most fascinating and in-depth article.

• Bear in mind that very few trips ever end up entirely free and (even without the mini-bar raids) assignments featuring five-star hotels or chic safari lodges can run up more in tips alone than you might budget for if you were simply paying the going rate for less salubrious accommodation.

In short, unless the trip is absolutely irresistible, we tend to avoid group press trips. Ideally, if you can get a reputation as a widely published and prolific writer, you have excellent appeal anyway as a candidate for a far more exclusive solo press trip.

THE BENEFITS OF SOLO PRESS TRIPS

When PR organisations learn that you have two or three good commissions confirmed, most will consider it worthwhile hosting you for a solo trip. In this case you sidestep the limitations (and the added competition) of a formal group press trip. An even more beneficial aspect is that your PR contact is now normally able to tailor the trip towards the specific angles you want to cover.

Take the reputation as a widely published writer another step farther and you'll find that even a single decent commission is often enough to snag a press trip. There will come a time when you have a network of reputable PR professionals who understand that it is your business to produce stories as widely as possible and in the most prestigious titles you can reach. (This is, after all, how you pay your bills.) By that time you'll find that setting up a trip becomes much easier and, in the best-case scenario, a single quick email to the right person can set up an entire assignment.

Been there, says Mark...

In 2017 I was commissioned, at very short notice, to fly to Uganda to do a big feature on bark cloth (the traditional craft of creating cloth from the bark of fig trees). It would be a long way to go for just one story but I knew a very helpful and super-efficient PR contact who had a network of clients in the country. She was aware that I'd be chasing other stories too, and so was able to set up a three-week trip up at zero expense. I covered the bark-cloth story and also racked up enough extra safari material for what finally amounted to 11 other full-length magazine features and a chapter for a coffee-table book called Best Moment of My Life.

Of course, the more prolific you are as a writer the more in-demand you will be, and the more likelihood there is that you'll be approached by PR organisations who are interested in having you write about their clients. The International Travel Writers Alliance (www.internationaltravelwritersalliance.com) sends a monthly newsletter out to its members with press releases from PR companies who are actively seeking travel journalists with the potential to write about their clients.

ONGOING PARTNERSHIPS

I hesitate to use the word 'partnership' here since it implies a level of give-and-take between a writer and a hosting tourism organisation. In reality, the writer is merely being offered ongoing opportunities to experience the product. Just as the freelance writer is only as good as the last article written, the hosting organisation is only as good as the last successful trip. They must accept that the writer will report honestly each and every time.

Nevertheless, there is mutual benefit in 'partnering' a prolific writer with a reputable travel company.

Without ever influencing how features are written, that company can help to put the writer into a position to secure a whole string of publishable features. And – as long as the product remains recommendable – the writer is ethically bound to tell the truth and say so.

There can be nothing unethical about such 'partnerships' as long as the travel writer is committed to honest reporting and the 'sponsor' does not try to influence positive exposure. There have been cases when I've turned down highly appealing trips if a hosting company expects a sworn commitment to positive exposure even prior to departure.

The number-one responsibility for any journalist (in any field) should always be to *tell it like it is*.

§

11

TIPS FOR GETTING
YOUR PHOTOS PUBLISHED

by Mark Eveleigh

*If you want to be a better
photographer, stand in front of
more interesting stuff.*

– Jim Richardson –

If you've read this book from the beginning, you've (hopefully) picked up some pointers on the life choices and business practises that will put you in front of 'more interesting stuff'. It's not *crucial* that you should be a photographer if you want to establish yourself as a professional travel writer, but (even apart from the added income) it certainly helps.

Let's say you've just trail-blazed a journey to a previously unexplored region or researched the most enigmatic and astounding cultural story on a little-known community. You're now trying to convince an editor to commission your once-in-a-lifetime story about a subject that's never previously been written about. But there's a problem; you're not a photographer, and since the region was unexplored (or the community virtually unknown) it's never been photographed. It's *extremely* unlikely that your story will ever see the light of day.

It's not necessary to set yourself up to compete with *National Geographic*'s finest shooters, but if you take Jim Richardson's advice and 'stand in front of stuff that's interesting enough' there's every chance that your photos could be used to illustrate your own stories. Although you should strive for excellence in both writing and shooting, bear in mind that a wonderfully written story can sometimes carry an article despite lack of great images, just as the most beautiful shots are frequently used to camouflage lacklustre copy.

HOW TO SELL MORE PHOTOS

This is not the place to present a crash-course on the technicalities of photography. Let's assume you own a camera and are proficient at pointing it at 'interesting stuff' and clicking the shutter. Don't imagine at this stage that you need to compete with the entire army of travel photographers out there who have dedicated their entire career to capturing world-class images. As the writer of the travel feature, you're naturally already in prime position to get images published to illustrate that feature.

Your best bet is to write your photos into the story. Deliberately work in incidents or moments that are represented in the best of your images. There are countless ways in which you can do this, and the following examples will probably bring to mind other possibilities that might fit better with your style or the type of feature you want to craft.

QUOTE SOMEONE YOU'VE PHOTOGRAPHED

A direct quote from an interesting character will make your portraits suddenly more appealing to a picture editor. It's unlikely that competing photographers will have images of that same person, so consider weaving that character more intricately into your story.

WRITE ABOUT AN INCIDENT YOU CAPTURED

A dramatic incident that happened to you personally might form the crux (or just the intro) of your story. It stands to reason that you're likely to be the only person who has images to illustrate that particular event. In this case you're already in a great position to get your shot into print.

KEYWORD YOUR IMAGES

When you label and keyword your photographs use careful and accurate keywording to ensure that an editor always knows what they are looking at. The sort of quirky image that might pique a reader's curiosity can be sold based on descriptive keywords (which have – as with everything else you write – been fact-checked and checked for spelling errors).

CAPTION YOUR IMAGES

As a travel writer, take pride in your captions – good captions can sell images… or at least put you a solid step ahead of the vast majority of photographers (and even established image banks) who habitually underestimate the importance of captioning.

KIT LIST FOR TRAVEL PHOTOGRAPHERS

Photography is about compromise. You balance aperture with shutter speed. You balance fading light with the need to avoid camera-shake. In travel photography you balance a desire for the equipment you need to capture stunning images with the need to travel as lightly as possible.

If you're a *National Geographic* assignment shooter with a personal assistant and an excess-baggage allowance that covers a shipping-container full of Pelican cases, you can skip this section. Let's assume, however, that you're just a regular freelancer on the threshold of a big trip and you'd like to come back with a reasonable selection of publishable images. The following tips will help you get the best out of your photography, even if you're not Ansel Adams.

CHOOSE YOUR CAMERA BAG WISELY

The array of camera bags, backpacks and hold-alls on offer can be confusing. Simplify things by making a choice between two basic alternatives. If you carry a lot of equipment and enjoy spending time setting up the right shot and selecting accessories, then a specially designed camera pack with compartments could be perfect for you. If, however, you want to be able to react quickly, to grab your camera and shoot on the move, then you'll need something you can carry over one shoulder. (Over the course of time the pay-off will probably be a bad back. Live with it – most pro travel photographers do).

AVOID BRANDED CAMERA BAGS

Camera bags with a manufacturer's logo branded on them advertise expensive contents to hustlers and thieves who might covet your prized Nikon/Canon hardware.

BE PREPARED FOR RAIN AND RIVERS

Take a waterproof stuff-sack if you're going anywhere near water. You can buy these roll-top canoeist bags in almost any travel store and they are a must-buy bargain at any backpacker ghetto from Istanbul to Bangkok. Think of these bags as the next best thing to travel insurance. The last time I decided it wasn't worth taking one was the day that *two* of my cameras ended up at the bottom of a river in Mexico.

TRAVEL WITH A CARABINER

Take a carabiner so that you can hook your camera onto the shoulder strap of your pack when you're hiking. During a long trek you'll appreciate the fact that, even while the camera remains to hand, the weight is removed from your neck or hands. (It also prevents you from dropping the camera, even if you slip.)

PACK A LIGHT-WEIGHT TRIPOD

The standard advice is that you need a heavy tripod to cut down on vibrations, especially on windy days. But for the demands of most travellers there are ways to get around the disadvantages of a light tripod, which you can either fly with or buy (cheaply) upon arrival.

Even the most basic models often have a hook underneath from which you can hang a weight: your own camera bag is frequently sufficient, but you could take a net bag (less wind resistance) that you can weigh down with a rock. If your tripod doesn't have a hook use your carabiner to add a weight to your tripod.

CARRY A LENS POUCH

A big lens pouch is useful for keeping equipment

instantly accessible. Get one with a Velcro belt strap so that you can fasten it to your belt when you're trekking.

WEAR CLOTHES WITH DEEP POCKETS

Cargo pants or bush shorts with big side pockets that are large enough to take a regular lens might be the most useful purchase you'll make for your trip.

TRAVEL WITH TWO CAMERA BODIES

Travelling light is always a good thing but if you're going on safari, for example, or travelling in dusty regions then consider taking two camera bodies. Your camera's sensor will be far better protected if you don't need to change lenses while jolting along a dirt track through a sandstorm in an open Land Rover. Also, with one camera permanently fitted with a telephoto lens and the other with a wide-angle, you're always ready to react instantly to that split-second photo opportunity.

KEEP A SHOWER CAP IN YOUR BAG

Many people think that shower caps were invented to keep your hair dry in the shower – but the best use for one of those super-lightweight, flimsy little disposable shreds of elasticated plastic is as an instantly accessible rain-cover for your camera. (You can buy a Nikon branded rain-cover for about US$15… or just keep the shower caps that are provided for free in hotel bathrooms.)

TRUST YOUR INNER ARTIST

Regardless of what sort of camera you are using – a top of the range DSLR or a simple point-and-shoot – don't forget to take your own creativity on the trip with you. Read the instruction manual, learn how your camera works so that you can operate most functions in the dark. And ignore the auto mode. The camera hasn't been invented that is more imaginative than an artistic eye. Don't let your camera tell you how you should capture that unforgettable moment: you tell it!

Been there, says Narina...

I once worked on a magazine where, on every assignment, our editor expected us to travel with two camera bodies, three lenses, a flash, spare batteries, a heavy tripod and numerous rolls of film. It might be as a response to this that nowadays I'm often tempted to explore a new city or market with my smartphone as my only camera.

What I find invaluable when I do this (or, when I stick my hand over the edge of a boat or out of a window to take a photo) is the wrist-lanyard that is attached to the cover of my phone. It's a simple, under-rated piece of gear that's becoming more and more difficult to find.

THE IMAGES YOU SHOULD CAPTURE

This is not a book on how to shoot travel photos. Let's assume you understand how your camera works… and you might even have gone so far as to read the manual. So, you know basically how to point and shoot. Even better, you understand the meaning of that all-important relationship between the shooting speed (or the ISO), aperture and depth of field (F-number).

Now, study the publication you're working for. What sort of shots do they prefer?

THE HERO SHOT

Many publications habitually favour a glorious DPS (double-page spread) to open the feature. If so, it will probably be balanced with some neutral space as an inset for the title and blurb (sky, maybe, or out-of-focus background). If the magazine pays according to size, this shot alone might boost your fee by as much as 50%. So, don't turn it down. (Beginner tip: a relatively low F-number and a longer lens both help to throw the background out of focus.)

MAIN SUBJECTS

Does the publication tend to prefer portraits of people, wide landscapes or lifestyle shots of travellers living the dream? Focus on those angles. As with your writing though, don't be so tied up in delivering the standard fare that you refuse to experiment.

IMAGES OF DETAILS

Always be on the lookout for interesting detail shots, such as hands engaged in work or crafts, soft-focus details of books or drinks on a table, artistic angles of traditional jewellery, an animal's eye rather than the entire beast. The possibilities are endless, but these little space-fillers (frequently able to stand alone on the page without the need for a caption) can turn out to be exactly what's needed at the layout stage when the design team are slotting images and text together.

Been there, says Narina...

When I'm feeling creatively stuck, when I'm just not 'seeing' interesting things to photograph, I like to set myself a mini theme-based assignment. I'll challenge myself to walk around a city and, for an hour, shoot only things that are blue, for example, or that contain only numbers, or textures, or reflections. Putting these boundaries in place channels my focus and helps me to find new ways of 'seeing'... and inspiration comes rushing back.

HOW TO PROCESS YOUR IMAGES

There are as many ways to work as there are professional photographers but, after much trial and error, this has become my ideal processing system:

SHOOT — A LOT

There's more to being a great photographer than just shooting endless images until a goodie eventually pops up. It can also be a numbers game, nevertheless. The legendary photographic superstars of the film age were famously free to burn through endless rolls of film while their competitors had to count costs-per-click. In the digital era an extra shot costs nothing. (I frequently shoot upwards of 2,000 images on a three-day assignment and I'm willing to bet that the final selection would be markedly less impressive had I shot only 200.)

SHOOT IN RAW FORMAT

Some of the top publications (*National Geographic,* for example) habitually demand to see RAW files to make sure that the photographer hasn't made excessive changes. You can always downsize your images once you've edited them.

EDIT THE SELECTION

Bin the duds but don't be too strict. You never know if something specific might later be requested and having found it among your files, you can bag another valuable sale. (Since my first assignment with a digital camera in 2004 I've racked up 55,000 fully polished and captioned shots, but I also have another 100,000 unpolished RAW files backed up on my hard drives.)

CONVERT TO JPEG

Copy the selection of what you consider to be publishable shots into a separate file (this is yet another backup) then convert the entire batch into maximum resolution Jpegs. (Some professional photographers prefer Tiffs, but I've never met a picture editor who wouldn't accept Jpegs.)

POLISH THE JPEGS AND TWEAK LEVELS

I use Adobe Photoshop. It's just a question of habit but I'm so familiar with the tools that I'd never switch to anything else. (Whichever editing program you use, be sure to learn those wonderful, time-saving hot-keys.)

How you polish the shots is a matter of taste, but the absolute basics for most photographers include 'topping-and-tailing' (adding contrast by making the whites a touch lighter and the blacks darker), perhaps a touch of saturation and the removal of any imperfections like dust-specks on the sensor.

ADD CAPTIONS

Write captions and keywords into the IPTC fields (usually just called file info). I use Adobe Bridge, for the reasons mentioned above. This step is arguably even more important than the polishing and I make sure I do it early in the image-preparation process so that every copy of an image that is made from this stage onwards will always carry the captions and keywords. Furthermore, they will usually be imported automatically into most online lightbox sites.

SAVE LOW-RES VERSIONS

One last thing to do – bulk process for a separate selection of low-resolution Jpegs (which, as explained above, will already have their captions and keywords imported without any extra input from you). These can be used for online publications – or for your own social media. Most importantly, they can be used in a sample low-res lightbox, an incredibly valuable hook since you can use it to include a sneak-peek when you pitch. (Heads-up for an editorial pet hate – don't trip yourself up by spelling it 'sneak-peak'.)

HOW TO SUBMIT YOUR IMAGES

Your priority should be to make it as easy as possible for picture editors to access and use your images. I upload the high-resolution Jpeg images to Google Drive (there are many other options that are equally as good) and I also upload a full selection of low-res images to a lightbox on Smugmug.com. Be sure, however, that such lightboxes are not open to public viewing since editors prefer that the images they are offered have previously seen as little exposure as possible. For this reason, you might want to resist uploading your greatest, most publishable masterpieces to Instagram or Facebook before you submit them to an editor.

IS PROFESSIONAL TRAVEL PHOTOGRAPHY STILL A VIABLE BUSINESS?

Are you a writer who shoots or a photographer who writes? If you really want to make a viable income out of freelancing for magazines and newspapers, these are really your only two options. Maximise your publishing potential and your income by doing both.

Been there, says Mark…

I'm definitely a 'writer who shoots'. If pushed I tend to describe myself as 60% writer and 40% photographer. Throughout the first decade of my career my income spreadsheets represented this balance almost exactly (and I probably made around 300 photo sales each year).

Most freelance photographers I know complain that over the last few years rates have been slipping across the board. My own spreadsheets would seem to back this up: by 2017 that typical 60/40 balance had slipped so that I was only making 30% of my annual income through photography; by 2019 it had slipped farther to less than 25%.

DON'T LOSE FOCUS

The legendary conflict photographer Sir Don McCullin once explained that there was no great mystery to the photographic art: 'F8 and be there,' he quipped.

My old friend Steve Davey, a highly experienced photographer who has worked on several BBC books (among much else), once summed up the challenges faced by assignment photographers about as succinctly as I've ever heard it put. 'Given enough time, good light and beautiful surroundings any muppet can go out and get a handful of good shots,' he said. 'A talented assignment shooter is the one who goes out with a tight deadline, in bad conditions, in unphotogenic surroundings and – through sheer determination and imagination – *still* delivers.'

THE BIGGER PICTURE

Narina once wrote a short piece she called 'life lessons from a camera bag'. There are some pretty useful points in there – particularly the last one.

• Choose your perspective carefully. It will influence the way you see the world.

• There is beauty in everything. If you can't see it, move from where you stand.

• Everybody sees a different picture.

• Be patient.

• Be impulsive.

• Every photograph tells a story. You choose that story and how it's told.

• It is often the grittiest subjects – not the most beautiful – that make the most interesting photographs.

• To get a clearer picture, you might need to change your perspective.

• Never forget to look up.

• And remember to look down.

• Sometimes you're so busy trying to capture the moment, you forget to live it. Put your camera away sometimes – you'll create your own very special memories.

12

HOW TO TRAVEL
LIKE A PRO

by Mark Eveleigh

*It is often safer to be in chains than
to be free.*

– Franz Kafka –

The more you travel, the longer your list of travel tips is likely to become. How useful some of those tips are to others will often depend entirely on personal preference – for example, the best place to sit on a plane, and what things to never travel without (Narina swears by tea tree oil, charcoal tablets and a sarong; I'd go with hammock, waterproof bag and Tabasco). Other tips are far more practical…

HOW TO SURVIVE THE FIRST 40 MINUTES IN A NEW CITY

The world is populated with wonderfully hospitable, friendly and delightful people. Unfortunately, our first experience of any new destination is normally the frantic arrivals terminal of an international airport. Every country has its share of con-artists and hustlers and they all know that airports are the best hunting grounds for naïve new arrivals.

Once you're clear of the airport your chances of getting ripped off are drastically reduced. Whether you're a first-time gap-year backpacker or an experienced globe-trotter, here are some hard-won tips to help you get through the crucial first 40 minutes.

SET YOUR WATCH

Jetlag is for amateurs. The moment the plane takes off set your watch to local time at destination – and don't let flight attendants confuse you by serving breakfast at 10pm or G&Ts at 7am. (I'm not saying you necessarily need to *refuse* the G&T, in fact there's something delightfully decadent about drinking a post-take-off G&T while trying to convince yourself that it's breakfast time.)

If you concentrate on getting your body-clock synchronized into your new time-zone as fast as possible, the worst symptom you'll suffer will be the natural mild fatigue of a long journey and a disturbed night. Follow this simple tip and you need never again suffer the full-blown 3am wakefulness of jetlag.

KEEP TRACK OF YOUR TRAVEL DOCUMENTS

Email yourself a security sheet that contains the details of your credit cards, as well as airline bookings and travel insurance details. Keep them scanned on your phone too so that even if you lose everything you can still access the important information you need.

Leave copies of flight details and travel insurance with family so that somebody is always up to date with your itinerary.

Upload a scan of your passport to your laptop and phone too. (This saved me a lot of time and bureaucratic stress in Guatemala City when I had to replace a stolen passport that had been swiped from my bag while I was almost unconscious with a fever).

BOOK A FLIGHT THAT LANDS EARLY

When you're booking flights, plan to arrive early in the day. A morning arrival leaves you with ample time to negotiate the transfer to your hotel or onward travel. Arriving late at night adds to the pressure and leaves you feeling disoriented in a city you don't know and can barely even see.

Also, some airports have less security on patrol at

night and taxis or buses are likely to be erratic. Likewise, book the departure flight for the afternoon so that there's no rush to get to the airport.

BOOK A HOTEL WITH BENEFITS

If budget allows, consider spending your first night in a new city at a hotel that offers an airport shuttle. It's very reassuring to have somebody meet you at arrivals with a big smile and your name written on a card.

An upgraded hotel also gives that feeling of security, buying you an extra day or two in which to find your feet and learn the ropes in a new city.

DITCH YOUR BAGGAGE TAGS

Those baggage tags looped into your luggage speak loud-and-clear to every hustler in the city: 'JOJ!' they scream (Just off the Jet), or 'FOB!' (fresh off the boat). You might as well scrawl NAÏVE across your forehead in permanent marker.

Some airports have staff at the exit cross-referring passengers with their baggage but, once you're sure you're beyond the final checkpoint, lose the evidence as fast as possible and try to look like you've been around for ages.

RESEARCH BEFORE YOU LEAVE HOME

Hustlers are looking for people who hesitate, wear a bemused expression or have a brand-new guidebook gripped in white-knuckled fingers. Try to get enough prior information so that you can look confident upon arrival and keep moving decisively. No two airports have the same transportation system so if in doubt tag on behind travellers who look local and follow their cue. Or queue.

USE THE DOMESTIC TERMINAL

Many major international airports also have a domestic terminal attached. Freed from the betraying evidence of those international baggage tags, you're likely to find that the domestic terminal is infinitely less stressful… and is a less likely honeypot for hustlers.

If you've arrived early and have time to kill at the airport, this terminal might be the best area in which to wait: café prices are often more representative of local norms and even taxis often cost less from this side.

TAKE YOUR TIME

Don't get caught up in the must-exit-the-airport rush. The best way to spend the first hour in a new country is often simply to find a quiet café table from which to check the lay of the land. Just sit and people-watch while you make a plan.

There's the added benefit that anyone who might be 'people-watching' you will get the impression that you're relaxed and in control of the situation, and they will go to look for easier pickings elsewhere.

KEEP ON TOP OF YOUR FINANCES

Don't forget to alert your bank to the fact that you'll be travelling so that your cards function. It helps to arrive with some cash in the local currency so that you don't have to stop at an airport ATM. (Juggling bags while fiddling with a wallet and credit cards is a recipe for disaster).

Memorise the exchange rate before you arrive and have an idea of what your airport transport is likely to cost. Once you have local cash familiarise yourself with the notes: you don't want to pay 10-times the going rate for an airport taxi simply because you thought you were handing over purple 10,000 rupiah notes when you were actually showering the driver with pretty pink 100,000s.

CARRY TWO CREDIT CARDS

Carry *at least* two credit cards, stashed in separate bags. Don't get stranded simply because your only card was stolen, lost or eaten by a machine. One of the accounts should be loaded only with minimal funds and topped up as needed so that you have a card to use anywhere you think security might be compromised (handy for online purchases too).

Have a backup plan in place so that family or friends can wire funds in a worst-case scenario. There are many pre-loaded debit cards specifically geared towards travellers. (Wise – originally called TransferWise – allows you to withdraw from ATMs all over the world while only paying local charges. It is also phenomenally useful for transferring funds internationally).

LEARN THE LANGUAGE

In many countries where haggling is the norm the mere ability to be able to ask the price in a local language (and to understand the reply) can snag you a 30% discount on the starting price. Speaking a few words in the local language will give the impression that you know your way around but, most importantly, it shows the level of respect you have for your hosts.

USE A LEGIT TAXI SERVICE

At airports take the official taxis rather than the random 'guys with cars' who haunt arrival areas. If you're staying in a ritzy hotel and don't want to get ripped off for the taxi fare, tell the driver you are going to somewhere '*near* the Ritz/Mandarin/Sheraton…' when you're haggling. (Likewise, when leaving the hotel don't ask the doorman to hail a limo. Instead, stroll a block away from the lobby before you look for a taxi).

Alternatively, just use Uber or Grab. These apps have brought a sort of democracy back to the world of taxis with rates that are the same whether you're a local, an expat or a greenhorn tourist.

A couple of years ago we were commissioned to spend several months researching a book on Bangkok's 'secret-spots', and Grab (Asia's equivalent of Uber) turned out to be invaluable in getting us to unpronounceable locations that were totally unknown even to Thai taxi drivers and taxi-motorbike riders. Grab's pin-drop system at the booking stage meant that there was no need even to explain where we wanted to go, no need to agree a price for each ride (locals and foreigners are charged alike) and no need to hand over cash or search for change since the charge can be linked directly to a credit card.

Very reassuring security benefits also lie in the fact that drivers have been vetted, your journey is tracked and there's even an emergency button on the app which you can hit if you think anything suspicious is going on.

WALK LIKE A LOCAL

If you are in a dodgy part of a potentially risky city carry your daypack under your arm rather than on your back, don't carry a guidebook in your hand, and don't stop to consult a map at every corner. Better to find a quiet spot, learn where you need to go and then walk with confidence.

THE TRAVEL ESSENTIALS

One of the most frequently used quotes – now a cliché – about travel is 'lay out all your clothes and all your money. Then take half the clothes and twice the money'. It's sound advice indeed, but here are a few things that you might never want to leave home without:

DURABLE LUGGAGE

Travelling as a journo in this gadget-heavy age means carrying a lot of equipment. Unless you're going to be actively trekking or on a seriously remote expedition, then consider leaving the backpack behind and travelling instead with a tough kitbag on wheels. Don't skimp on durability and get one with seriously sturdy wheels since that's what takes the hammering on rough village dirt-tracks and potholed city sidewalks.

A WELL-DESIGNED BAG

Choose a kitbag with a main zipped section that can be locked with a padlock. Usually, I tend to ignore hotel safes as you can rarely be sure who else has the key, and if it's a combination lock there is always an over-ride code. Instead, I lock my valuables in my kitbag. It's far from 100% secure but few opportunistic thieves will risk stealing or slashing a bag and you can see at a glance if anything has been touched.

If you're suspicious about unexpected visits to your room while you're out use the old private-eye trick and trap a small sliver of paper in the door when you lock it – that way you can see instantly if anyone was in your room while you were out.

A PADLOCK

Travel with a strong padlock with a clip that's long enough to go through a door latch. Some hotels will give you a padlock to lock your room, and sometimes for lockers. You never know who might have a spare key, so stow the padlock you were given at check-in and use your own.

HOW TO BECOME AN 'ADVENTURER'

'What I'm looking for,' someone once wrote in an email to me, 'is some advice on becoming, for lack of a better word, an Adventurer.'

It wasn't the sort of email you tend to get very often. Perhaps it was the inherent desperation in the way he'd capitalised Adventurer that convinced me that his email merited the most serious response I could give it.

I knew nothing about him beyond what I read in his email, but something had clearly pushed him to the verge of a big change in his life: 'Over the last several years I have undergone many personal life changing events and know first-hand, that life can change in an instant,' he said. 'I have come to the conclusion that it is time to put serious thought into following my dreams of adventure and travel. What I really want is advice on how to pursue a career and lifestyle as an Explorer.'

After a two-decade career as a professional traveller, I could offer some advice on the dog-eat-dog world of freelance photojournalism... but had little idea how to carve a lifestyle as an Explorer.

'I'm writing to you now because I have been a fan of yours for several years and I very much enjoy the work you have done,' he said. 'I want to do something similar.'

I thought back to the beginning in search of a clue that might help him. The hunger for travel that made me turn towards a career in full time travel-writing... and to the resulting poverty that that made adventurous travel a virtual impossibility for the first few years.

I thought back further. Before 'the beginning'. For a decade before I started writing professionally, I'd worked as a labourer, lorry driver or security guard to pay for long, seat-of-my-pants, back-to-basics trips to the remotest regions I could reach. I hitch-hiked everywhere and slept under bridges and on building-sites on four continents.

As far back as I could remember I'd wanted to be an Adventurer – or, rather, to live a life of adventure – but, like my friend, I'd had no idea how to achieve it. Freelance travel-writing was never my dream job, simply because I never dreamed that a job like this even existed.

And it struck me that the only advice I could offer to someone who wants to live a life of adventure is to do something *so incredibly different* that people have to notice. The biggest boost I had at the beginning of my career was my expedition through Central Borneo. After that I became (as far as I was aware) the first foreigner in 125 years to walk right across a section of Madagascar's 'Zone Rouge' bandit country.

I remember meeting a young motoring journalist who had made a similar discovery: he had won the world record for fastest driver blind-folded and for the most number of donuts in a minute. Because of this, magazines took an interest in him and editors began to commission him.

There are many paths to becoming a travel writer, as this book will already have shown. But for someone who wants to be an adventurer, or an explorer, there are other more frightening choices to make. Are you willing to take a couple of years out of your life to dedicate to a single mind-blowing trip? Research hard (I taught myself Indonesian for Borneo), prepare thoroughly and undertake the most recklessly exciting trip you can imagine. There are no prizes for second place so pick something completely original – and at least slightly insane. Something that nobody has ever done.

When you get back build on your own skills to turn the experience into a career. If you have that real love for writing then write. If you're an artist tell your stories through photography or painting. If you're a gifted speaker then use the inspiring tale of your travels to launch a career as a motivational speaker (and earn more in a single hour than you might in weeks as a writer).

The glory of that wild trip won't carry you forever and you will need to do something to follow up, but it could provide the momentum for your next ground-breaking trip. Do it enough times and before long you could be a professional Adventurer. And if it doesn't work...well, at least you made that one awesome, incredible, once-in-a-lifetime journey. And that's more than most people ever do.

The world is still an immensely big and wild place and the possibilities are endless. The only question now is: where do you want to go?

HOW TO GET OFF THE BEATEN TRACK

There's nowhere in the world that cannot be explored if you have the help of reliable local guides. Livingstone might have become the greatest name in the history of exploration, but he could not have done what he did without the help of his unshakable guides Chuma and Susi. Where would Hillary have been without Sherpa Tenzing or Lewis and Clarke without the fearless Indian woman Sacajawea?

Some of the most celebrated feats of exploration in history were only possible through the help of local guides. We know the names of a few of the most famous but in far too many cases these are the unsung heroes of early travel. An African classic I re-read recently carried a description of the writer as a safari pioneer on the back cover: 'Robert Ruark's first safari was in Kenya and Tanganyika, accompanied by only his wife, a white hunter and a staff of Africans…' That says it all.

I've mounted more than a dozen expeditions into uncharted (or barely explored) parts of Asia, Africa and Latin America. In every case these trips were only possible with the help of local guides – many of whom became lifelong friends. In areas with at least some tourist infrastructure there will be national park authorities or tourist information offices that can recommend guides. The following tips are from lessons I've learned (mostly the hard way) and relate to off-the-beaten-track locations where you'll have to find and hire your own expedition crew:

MEET WITH THE VILLAGE LEADER

The police force that's more effective than community or tribal law has yet to be formed. There are few better ways to find reliable guides than to ask a village headman to hand-pick them for you. A guide who's aware that he is custodian of the honour of his village – and that he will have to answer to tribal law should anything happen to you – is likely to be the most helpful and trustworthy you'll ever find.

DON'T RUSH THE DELICATE
PROCESS OF HAGGLING

In many traditional communities it is considered the height of bad manners to launch straight into business without the prerequisite period of chit-chat. Haggle reasonably firmly to fix the rate (always with good humour and a smile) but at the same time stipulate that a good bonus will be paid afterwards if you're thoroughly happy with how the trip went. This way you offer what is ultimately a fair/generous rate but tied to an incentive.

Beware that sometimes alcohol is a problem in traditional communities – if this is the case consider offering half the payment upfront prior to departure, and the rest on completion of the trek. This way there's a better chance that money will make it into the households rather than being frittered away in bars on return from a long, thirsty stint in the wilderness.

WHEN TO PAY UPFRONT

If you want to get from A to B with minimum delay then arrange to pay for the entire trip, rather than by the day. This can work best if, for example, provisions might be in short supply on the trail and you need to make the journey before food or water runs out.

WHEN TO PAY BY THE DAY

If, on the other hand, taking time to soak up the experience is the priority, then arrange to pay by the day. This way your guides will be in no hurry and (as long as you have necessary provisions) you can even extend the stay longer or be free to make detours. If you're paying by the day, make sure that your provisioning plans (and budget) take into account a longer stay than you originally envisaged.

BUDGET FOR A BONUS

Whether you pay up front or by the day, hold some of your budget back and make it known that there will be a bonus at the end 'if the trip goes well'. This can also be a great opportunity to find a new home for some of your clothing and kit that you might consider past their best but which might see another decade of use here in the wilds.

On one Central American jungle trip I welcomed a request from my lead guide to give his 10-year-old son a chance to experience the deep jungle. Wary of falling into the trap of hiring child labour I stipulated that the boy would not be working but that he was more welcome to come with us on 'vacation'. I was keen that he should have a chance to learn from the skills of the older tribesmen, but he proved himself so useful around camp and as a chef that I ended up wondering how I could justify paying him. Rather than give him cash I bequeathed the best piece of travel equipment I had; it was only afterwards that it occurred to me how incongruous it was to make a gift of a six-inch Toledo-steel bush-knife to a 10-year-old boy. (Even at his age he was more practised with a knife than I was and I have no doubt that that young man – now presumably in his twenties – still uses and prizes that knife.)

YOU MIGHT NEED TO TAKE A HUNTER

On longer expeditions it can be necessary to take a hunter with a gun. But if you really want him to be able to bring in meat you must be prepared to travel slower, allowing enough time for him to be able to hunt in the evenings or early morning. With a long, noisy column crashing through the bush you can't expect game to be easily visible.

It is very important to give strict guidelines as to what can and cannot be shot: I had to convince my Kuna guides in Darien that under no circumstances were they to shoot jaguar, and in a remote part of Kalimantan I was horrified to arrive in a Dayak hunters' camp just as the residents were finishing a feast of orangutan meat.

YOU MIGHT NEED ADDITIONAL GUIDES

If re-provisioning might be necessary part way through the trek, take extra guides. Few people will agree to walk solo through the jungle to carry provisions back from a village (and you can hardly blame them).

During an expedition in Chiapas we trekked through virtually unexplored jungle with guides (descendants of the Maya) who volunteered to shoot meat. Because of the area's protected status, however, I veto-ed that plan. So, we took extra porters in case a re-provisioning run back to a village was necessary. It wasn't necessary though because we also took a couple of live chickens that I slaughtered along the way for fresh meat.

LEARN THE LANGUAGE AND CULTURE

Before arrival in the country do your best to become at least slightly acquainted not only with the language, but with the lifestyle of the people in the area you'll be travelling through. Few pastoral people will be prepared to guide you (whatever incentive you're offering) during one of those crucial periods of the year when the herds/flocks need to be moved or the harvest is ready. This was a lesson that I learned the hard way when we arrived in central Borneo just as the rice was being harvested...and spent three fruitless weeks travelling between various jungle villages and longhouses, before I could entice anyone to guide us into the jungle.

YOUR GUIDES KNOW BEST

Listen to your guides when they advise what provisions are needed. In Asia few guides will be willing to travel without their pre-requisite ration of rice (frequently three plates each per day). In parts of Africa it might be mealie-meal/sadza/fufu/pap. In the Andes you will have little chance of getting together a team of mountain porters unless you budget for a sack of coca leaves. Hungry, disgruntled guides will not add to the experience on any expedition...and, in the worst scenarios, an expedition that is not functioning well as a team could potentially be dangerous.

DON'T SKIMP ON PORTERS

These days most travellers are aware of the plight of the overworked, overloaded and underpaid porters who have suffered in trekking destinations as far apart as the Annapurna Circuit, Kilimanjaro and the Inca Trail. Don't skimp on porters out of some misguided obligation that you must carry your own pack: the last person who will thank you for this is the poor soul who loses a good pay-packet because of your – albeit laudable – scruples.

For many years I refused to let a porter carry my kit. I was somewhere in the jungles of Sumatra when it dawned on me that for a few extra dollars – which one of the local men would be extremely grateful for – I was free to move with so much more agility. Loaded only with my camera equipment I was able to chase the shots and angles without the encumbrance of a heavy pack. I was free to do my job more effectively, and my hired porter was happy with an opportunity to do his.

§

WHAT EDITORS SAY
ABOUT THE AUTHORS

"I do love reading your stories – they've always got such a wonderful charm to them, and this piece is no different. I really enjoyed reading it, and you brought the village to life so well. Many thanks!"
– Editor, *BBC Travel*

"Thanks for such a great piece – it's something genuinely original, and a great read."
–Travel editor, *The Telegraph*

"What an exquisite story! You actually brought tears to my eyes. The beginning captures, the descriptions are wonderful, the story runs strongly all the way through, and then the end: moving. It makes me so happy to get work like this."
– Editor, *Getaway*

"I am really excited about this Serengeti article. What a beautiful trip, and what a great piece! Thanks for all the good work. Always a pleasure to work with you."
– Editor, KLM inflight magazine

"I really like your writing style – a rare gift!"
– Editor, *Private Edition*

"Love it. Storytelling as it should be. You've managed to deliver a really riveting read here. There are several brilliant lines, and your use of the first-person narrative is, well, first-class."
– Editor, Kenya Air inflight magazine

"A great read! Full of insight and colour."
– Editor, *BBC Wildlife*

"Thank you for the careful crafting of your Thailand and Greece features. I joined you freely on your trip to Chiang Mai, and imagined myself weaving through the busy streets in the back of a tuk-tuk. I loved the way you blended the ancient history with the modern familiarity in your Greece feature. I couldn't decide whether I wanted to wander around the ancient ruins or focus on the modern-day creative spirit and lifestyle. Sufficiently intrigued."
– Publisher, Ramsay Media

"I have just read your Zimbabwe copy. I think you have done a really excellent job. The structure works really

well, it's cogent and nicely written, and it's full of drama and intriguing observations. I'm very pleased with it."
–Deputy editor, *The Telegraph*

"I've come to consider you as a soldier of fortune or Legionnaire of the travel writing/photography business (please take it as a compliment!)"
– Editor, Korean Airlines inflight magazine

"An explosive opening followed by dripping-hot, immersive prose. I can really feel the power of your craft as I read this. I want this magazine to be a good read and this sort of work helps to ensure that it is."
– Editor, Kenya Airlines inflight magazine

"A borderline insane modern-day explorer."
– Editor, *Maxim*

§

If you enjoyed this book, please be sure to visit this book's Amazon page and drop a quick review. It really does mean a lot to writers.